SCIENCE
Superstars

SCIENCE SUPERSTARS. Copyright © 2021 by St. Martin's Press. All rights reserved. Printed in Singapore. For information, address St. Martin's Press, 120 Broadway, New York, NY 10271.

www.castlepointbooks.com

The Castle Point Books trademark is owned by Castle Point Publishing, LLC. Castle Point books are published and distributed by St. Martin's Publishing Group.

ISBN 978-1-250-27526-4 (paper over board)
ISBN 978-1-250-27527-1 (ebook)

Design by Katie Jennings Campbell
Edited by Monica Sweeney
Illustrations by Octavia Jackson
Inspiration for the portrait of Gertrude Caton Thompson used by permission. 400_036032 / 1938 © RAI

Our books may be purchased in bulk for promotional, educational, or business use. Please contact your local bookseller or the Macmillan Corporate and Premium Sales Department at 1-800-221-7945, extension 5442, or by email at MacmillanSpecialMarkets@macmillan.com.

First Edition: 2021

10 9 8 7 6 5 4 3 2 1

SCIENCE
Superstars

30 BRILLIANT WOMEN WHO CHANGED THE WORLD

JENNIFER CALVERT

illustrated by OCTAVIA JACKSON

CASTLE POINT BOOKS
NEW YORK

"DON'T LET ANYONE ROB YOU OF YOUR IMAGINATION,

your creativity, or your curiosity.

It's your place in the world;

IT'S YOUR LIFE.

Go on and do all you can with it,

and make it the life you want to live."

—MAE JEMISON, ASTRONAUT

CONTENTS

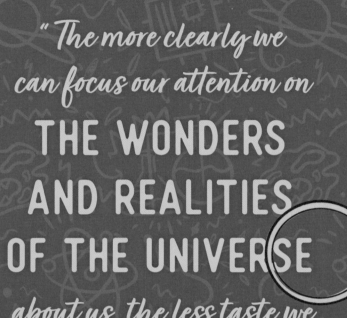

"*The more clearly we can focus our attention on* **THE WONDERS AND REALITIES OF THE UNIVERSE** *about us, the less taste we shall have for destruction.*"

—RACHEL CARSON, MARINE BIOLOGIST

INTRODUCTION

When you picture scientists, do you see beakers and lab coats? Maybe some complex equations scribbled in a notebook and samples squeezed under a microscope lens? It's time to zoom out on that image.

Add in the scuba divers and fossil collectors, not to mention the astronauts and inventors. Don't forget the doctors who treat us and the authors who inspire us. And, of course, the barefoot explorers who help us understand the natural world around us.

The truth is, science isn't just one thing. It's everything. It's how we understand our world, from the tiniest particles to the grandest galaxies. And it takes all of us—the doers, the designers, and especially the dreamers—to discover what the world is telling us. As chemist Stephanie Kwolek (page 89) put it, "All sorts of things can happen when you're open to new ideas and playing around with things."

Elizabeth Blackwell (page 17) and Jane Cooke Wright (page 77) set out to solve a problem and created space for women in medicine. Rachel Carson (page 53) and Jane Goodall (page 101) envisioned a world in harmony with nature and helped us understand our place in it. Katherine Johnson (page 73) and Vera Rubin (page 93) pushed past prejudice to explore space.

These are just a few of the many remarkable women who took science by storm by imagining the possibilities instead of settling for the status quo. Although they span dozens of specialties, all of these women have a few things in common: First, they embraced their curiosity. Second, they found joy in their work. And, third, they didn't let anything—not racism, sexism, ignorance, or even war—stand in their way.

It's amazing what a little curiosity can do when it's coupled with that kind of passion and determination. That's the stuff of scientific breakthroughs. So be curious. Dare to ask the big questions. Be open to the endless possibilities. The world is waiting for you to change it!

MARY ANNING

"I have always admired most those who lead with their eyes, like Mary Anning, for they seem more aware of the world and its workings."

—TRACY CHEVALIER

★ DISCOVERED NEVER-BEFORE-SEEN FOSSILS AND HELPED CHANGE THE WAY SCIENTISTS UNDERSTOOD EVOLUTION

★ HER DISCOVERIES CONTINUE TO BE DISPLAYED IN LONDON'S NATURAL HISTORY MUSEUM 200 YEARS LATER

When you think of quiet English towns, you probably don't picture dinosaurs roaming the countryside. But Lyme Regis in the southern seaside county of Dorset happened to be a hot spot for these prehistoric beasts and other long-extinct creatures. In fact, fossils were so prevalent in the area that people used to pluck them out of the sand like seashells as souvenirs. And until one smart, determined little girl came along, they had no idea of the history they were holding in their hands.

Mary Anning's father taught her to look for fossils on the beaches of Lyme Regis when she was just 5 years old. His job as a cabinetmaker didn't pay much, and selling these "curiosities" to tourists was a handy side hustle. But when her father died, that happy pastime became necessary to provide income for Mary, her brother Joseph, and their mom. Luckily, the Annings had a natural talent for discovery.

When Joseph came across a 4-foot-long fossilized skull in 1811, Mary immediately set out to find the rest of the enormous creature. She then spent months meticulously preparing what turned out to be the skeleton of a 17-foot monster that left scientists baffled. They called the Annings' discovery *ichthyosaurus*, or "fish lizard," and paid Mary's mom a tidy sum for the bones so they could study them.

At the time of the discovery, Georges Cuvier (the "father of paleontology") had only just introduced the theory of extinction. Many people still believed the Earth was only a few thousand years old. So, when they found the remains of a creature they couldn't identify, they just assumed it was still roaming the Earth somewhere. Thanks in part to Mary's discoveries of multiple ichthyosaurs, we now know the marine reptiles lived between 194 and 201 *million* years ago (and met their fate about 65 million years ago).

WHEN LIGHTNING STRIKES

When it comes to raising children today, everything from nutrition to TV time is up for debate. But in the early 19th century, parents were focused on keeping their kids alive. Nearly half of all children born in the United Kingdom died before the age of 5, many from diseases later eradicated by vaccines. Out of 10 siblings, only Mary and her brother Joseph made it to adulthood—and even that was a miracle. At least that's what the family's pastor called it when 15-month-old Mary survived being struck by lightning. Three others died, but Mary's health actually improved. Her parents even believed her precocious personality was a side effect of the strike.

Mary continued to navigate dangerous landslides in frigid winters (in heavy dresses, no less!) to discover and preserve fossils before they were washed out to sea. She unearthed creatures great and small, fish and mammal. One major discovery was a complete *Plesiosaurus* (another marine reptile) in 1823. Another was a mangled skeleton with wings and a long tail—the first pterosaur discovered outside Germany—in 1828.

Mary's expert fossil excavation and preparation, anatomical sketches, and scholarly identification made her the go-to girl among scientists in

LONDON Natural History Museum

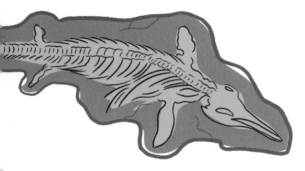

"*Mary Anning* [is] probably the most important unsung (or inadequately sung) collecting force in the history of paleontology."

—STEPHEN JAY GOULD

the field. They called her the "princess of paleontology." But that didn't earn her any official credit when the scientists published findings about her discoveries. After all, 19th-century England was a man's world.

Throughout her life, Mary was underpaid and underappreciated for her painstaking and dangerous work. And she wasn't happy about it. In fact, she wrote in one letter, "The world has used me so unkindly, I fear it has made me suspicious of everyone." She died from breast cancer in 1847 without ever seeing her true impact on scientists' understanding of evolution, extinction, and the history of our planet. Only after her death did we begin to learn how she paved the way for women in paleontology.

Mary was eulogized in the *Quarterly Journal of the Geological Society*, an organization that wouldn't even admit women until 1904. In 1865, legendary author Charles Dickens wrote an essay praising her for helping to create the newly formed science of geology. "The carpenter's daughter has won a name for herself, and has deserved to win it," Dickens wrote. In 2010, the Royal Society recognized her as one of the 10 most influential women scientists in British history. And today, people continue to flock to the Natural History Museum in London to see her discoveries, and to Dorset's "Jurassic Coast" to make their own.

CREDIT WHERE IT'S DUE

Rumor has it that Mary Anning was the real-life inspiration for Terry Sullivan's tongue twister, "She Sells Seashells by the Seashore." That may or may not be true, but the fact that so many believe it today tells you that Mary is finally getting the recognition she deserves for her incredible contributions to science.

MARIA MITCHELL

"We especially need imagination in science. It is not all mathematics, nor all logic, but it is somewhat beauty and poetry."

—MARIA MITCHELL

★ NOT ONLY THE FIRST FEMALE AMERICAN ASTRONOMER, BUT ALSO THE FIRST FEMALE ASTRONOMY PROFESSOR AND THE FIRST AMERICAN SCIENTIST TO DISCOVER A COMET

★ ADVOCATED FOR MATH AND SCIENCE EDUCATION FOR GIRLS WHEN FEW HAD ACCESS

The fact that Maria (pronounced Ma-RYE-ah) Mitchell discovered a comet may actually be the least interesting thing about her. But that's what happens when you buck the rules and fill your life with passion and purpose. Like a comet herself, the trail Maria blazed for others burned as brightly as her own accomplishments.

Like so many amazing young women, Maria had progressive parents to thank for encouraging her natural talents. Her dad, William (an amateur astronomer himself), nurtured Maria's love for math and science through nightly stargazing. But he also made sure she had the formal education she'd need to pursue a career in the field.

At the age of 12, Maria helped her dad calculate the position of their home by observing a solar eclipse. By 14, her exceptional calculations made her a sought-after navigator for whalers in Nantucket. And by 17, she had finished her formal education and opened a school of her own to train girls in math and science.

At 18, Maria slowed down for a bit. She worked as librarian of the Nantucket Atheneum by day and watched the skies with her dad at night. William had built an observatory on top of the Pacific

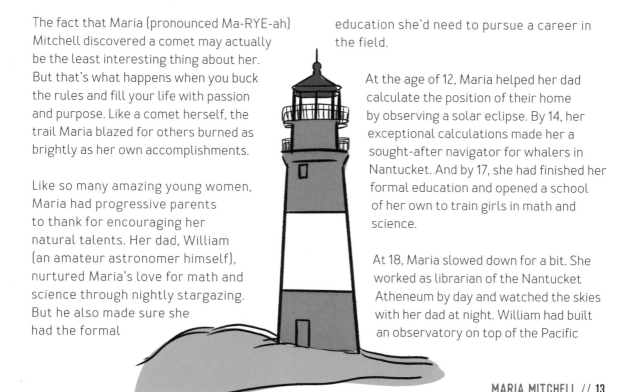

National Bank where he worked (a totally normal thing to do) and outfitted it with a 2-inch telescope. It was through that lens that Maria spotted a blurry blob of light that wasn't on any of her charts.

"Miss Mitchell's Comet," as it came to be known, earned 29-year-old Maria a gold medal from the King of Denmark and instant recognition from the scientific community. She became both the first woman elected to the American Academy of Arts and Sciences and the first to be admitted to the American Association for the Advancement of Science. After moving to Boston to work as a computer (mathematician) for the US government, Maria realized she wanted more.

So, 10 years after her big discovery, Maria traveled to Europe to meet with fellow astronomers at the great European observatories. With that renewed passion, Maria then accepted a teaching position at the newly founded Vassar College in Poughkeepsie, New York. The Vassar observatory was second only to Harvard's, and it felt like home to Maria. She quickly developed a reputation as a smart, sassy, and unconventional professor by scheduling classes at night and hosting mixers in the observatory that featured poetry and political speeches by famed feminists.

FIGHTING THE MAN

Society may not have seen women as equal to men while Maria was alive, but her family's Quaker faith did. And she instilled that sense of potential in every woman she met. Maria advocated for women's education by opening a training school and by teaching at Vassar. She advocated for women's equality by helping to establish the American Association for the Advancement of Women. And she advocated for women's independence by encouraging them to work in science, draw their own conclusions, and earn their own money. (She also advocated for herself when she found out that, at $800 a year, she was making a fraction of the salary given to male professors at Vassar.) In everything Maria did, she paved the way for other women to follow.

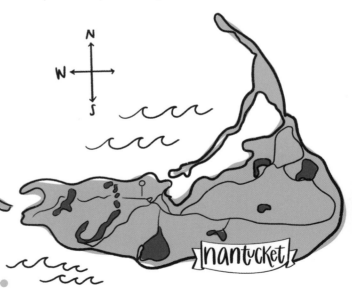

THE SLUG CLUB

Remember the Slug Club from *Harry Potter and the Half-Blood Prince*—that exclusive little circle of Professor Slughorn's most promising students? Maria beat him to it. Her group of rising stars (pun intended) was called the Hexagon, and it included future astronomer, supporter of women's rights, and Vassar professor Mary Whitney. Maria's teaching methods might have been unorthodox, but she certainly succeeded in empowering the next generation of female scientists. Many of her students were published in male-centric academic journals and three of her female mentees made the first list of Academic Men of Science in 1906.

Those quirky teaching methods proved to be pretty effective. As one of her students said, "A chance meeting with Miss Mitchell . . . gave one always an electric shock. At the slightest contact, a spark flashed." Maria lived to inspire that spark in her female students.

Maria believed that women, with their creativity and focus, were made for science. And she hated seeing them waste their talents on "domestic duties" like cleaning and sewing. As she put it, "Better to be peering in the spectrograph than on the pattern of a dress." So, Maria made it her mission to steer her students toward careers in science, not just for their benefit but for the benefit of the field.

Maria worked until she couldn't work anymore, dying just a year after retiring from Vassar. While she certainly had a love of both science and teaching, it was her passion for women's achievement that drove her to accomplish so much in her lifetime. And luckily for us, passion like that is contagious.

Vassar Observatory

ELIZABETH BLACKWELL, MD

"It is not easy to be a pioneer—but oh, it is fascinating! I would not trade one moment, even the worst moment, for all the riches in the world."

—ELIZABETH BLACKWELL

★ BECAME THE FIRST FEMALE PHYSICIAN IN THE UNITED STATES AND PIONEERED THE EDUCATION OF WOMEN IN MEDICINE

★ FOUNDED A HOSPITAL AND A COLLEGE, BOTH OF WHICH HAVE EVOLVED INTO HIGHLY RESPECTED INSTITUTIONS TODAY

Some people have the good fortune to know exactly what they want to do with their lives. They have vision, drive, and natural talent—it's like they were tailor-made for it. Elizabeth Blackwell was not one of those people. But once she figured out what was important to her, she didn't let anything stand in her way. (And for a woman in the early 1800s, that's saying something!)

Elizabeth's story began with a happy childhood in Bristol, England. But a few years after the family moved to America to find opportunity, they found hardship instead. In 1838, Elizabeth's father died and left her mother with no money and nine mouths to feed. But the Blackwells were made of tough stuff.

The older girls and their mom took up teaching to pay the bills, even opening their own school. With Elizabeth's love of learning, education seemed to suit her. But she never could have guessed that she would one day transform the field and change the face of medicine.

Mary Donaldson was dying of uterine cancer, and she asked her friend Elizabeth a simple question: "Why not study medicine?" The reason for the question was anything but simple. "If I could have been treated by a lady doctor," Mary said, "my worst sufferings would have been spared me." Mary had been belittled and mistreated by her male doctors—something that still happens to women today.

At first, Elizabeth shrugged off the idea. "I hated everything connected with the body and could not bear the sight of a medical book," she wrote in her autobiography, *Pioneer Work in Opening the Medical Profession to Women*. But she couldn't shake what Mary had said. In 1849, Elizabeth became the first female physician in America.

It may have taken only a few years, but it was an uphill climb. Elizabeth had applied to more than 20 medical schools and had been rejected by each one for lack of a Y chromosome.

Medicine was a man's business. It took a physician friend who had some pull at Geneva Medical College in upstate New York and a vote by the entirely male student body to get her foot in the door.

Elizabeth learned that her classmates had voted her in as a practical joke. Never did they imagine that she'd actually attend. When she did, the students shunned her, and the professors tried to have her barred from lessons. They were dumbstruck when Elizabeth graduated at the top of her class.

Unfortunately, sexism and ignorance were waiting for her outside of school as well. Elizabeth discovered she was unwelcome at most hospitals. But that didn't stop her. Instead, she started her own clinic and treated anyone who needed help, including those who were equally unwelcome in other hospitals.

TRAILBLAZING RUNS IN THE FAMILY

Elizabeth's good fortune was to be born into a family that believed in challenging the norm. Her father fought to end slavery and believed that his daughters should have the same opportunities as his sons. Elizabeth's brother and his wife fought to give women the right to vote. Another sister-in-law became the first female minister ordained in a mainstream Protestant denomination. And Elizabeth's sister Emily followed in her footsteps, becoming a surgeon and helping Elizabeth start her all-female hospital. That's some pretty impressive DNA!

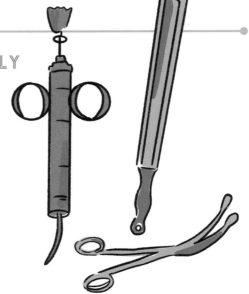

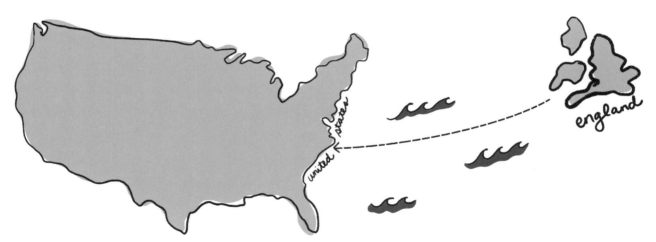

When women began to follow in Elizabeth's footsteps and head to medical school, she realized they would need a place to practice. So, in 1857, she opened the first hospital staffed entirely by women—the New York Infirmary for Indigent Women and Children. Today, that hospital is the highly respected New York-Presbyterian Lower Manhattan Hospital.

But Elizabeth knew firsthand that women also needed more inclusive instruction. That's why, in 1868, she opened the first medical college dedicated to training female physicians. Thirty years later, that college joined what is today the acclaimed Weill Cornell Medicine.

Elizabeth clearly believed that when you see a need, you fill that need. Because of her passion and determination, millions of patients received the care they needed. And because of

UP CLOSE AND PERSONAL

In between opening her own hospital and starting her own medical school, Elizabeth joined the war effort. She coordinated battlefield training for nurses and the collection of supplies. That effort evolved into the United States Sanitary Commission, which was approved by President Abraham Lincoln himself. In a letter to her adopted daughter, Kitty, Elizabeth described meeting the president at the White House. Her insightful takeaway? That Honest Abe was much uglier in person!

her vision, women now outnumber men in medical schools across the country. So, if you're not one of the lucky few who know exactly what to do with their lives, consider doing this instead: find a need, and take one small step toward filling it. You never know what could happen!

ELIZABETH GARRETT ANDERSON, MD

"When I felt rather overcome with my father's opposition, I said as firmly as I could, that I must have this or something else, that I could not live without some real work."

—ELIZABETH GARRETT ANDERSON

★ NOT JUST THE FIRST REGISTERED FEMALE PHYSICIAN IN BRITAIN BUT ALSO THE FIRST FEMALE DEAN OF A BRITISH MEDICAL SCHOOL AND THE FIRST FEMALE MAYOR IN BRITAIN

★ FOUGHT FOR WOMEN'S EQUALITY IN BOTH MEDICINE AND POLITICS

It's no coincidence that Elizabeth Blackwell and Elizabeth Garrett Anderson are twinning here. Sometimes, you find greatness on your own. Other times, you're inspired to it. And if you're really lucky, your journey is made a little easier by following in someone else's footsteps. For Elizabeth Garrett, the path was marked by Dr. Blackwell's hurried footprints.

Elizabeth Garrett met Dr. Elizabeth Blackwell when she was just a teenager. Pursuing a career in medicine hadn't even occurred to Elizabeth, but something about Dr. Blackwell stuck with her. It didn't thrill her parents quite as much. Her dad called the idea "disgusting," and her mom told her it was a disgrace. Thankfully, Newson Garrett ultimately decided to help his daughter follow her dreams. (Her mom mostly complained to relatives.)

None of the Garretts could have imagined the fight they had ahead of them. Like Dr. Blackwell, Elizabeth had to navigate sexism, ignorance, and sabotage to get her medical degree. But she had even more hoops to jump through. For one thing, absolutely none of the schools in Britain would admit her—not even as a joke.

Elizabeth settled on a 6-month trial as a nurse, but she couldn't help herself. She started attending lectures and treating patients with the male medical students. Although she wasn't officially allowed into the program, no one seemed to mind her sitting in. Until she aced the exams, that is. Suddenly, the male students were drawing up a petition calling Elizabeth a distraction and demanding she be expelled. And so she was.

That didn't stop Elizabeth. She discovered a loophole—a certification program that allowed any qualified "person" to apply. Of course, "person" didn't mean "woman." But thanks to Elizabeth, her father, and her father's lawyers, she was able to claw her way into the Society of Apothecaries and earn her license to practice. (The Society immediately changed the program's language to ensure that no other women could follow.)

Now, with license in hand, Elizabeth was ready to practice. In 1866, she took a page out of her hero's handbook and started her own dispensary (which is like a pharmacy crossed with a clinic). In 1872, St. Mary's Dispensary outgrew

A FEMINIST IN LOVE

Elizabeth met her husband, James Anderson, at the East London Hospital in 1870. Her friends were afraid she would give up her incredible career for domestic life, which was common in those days. But Elizabeth saw herself as an inspiring example to others that a woman could have both: a family and a career. It didn't hurt that James was in awe of his wife's accomplishments and supported her dreams completely. Theirs was a true partnership.

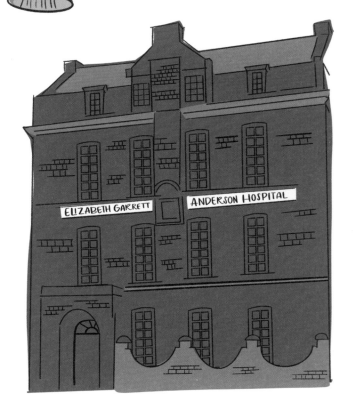

IN HER SPARE TIME

As if Elizabeth didn't have enough on her plate with running a hospital and a medical college, she also raised three children and fought for women's rights. Furthermore, she won a seat on the London School Board in 1870, the same year she received her MD in Paris. (That meant commuting by train from London to Paris to pass her final exams and defend her thesis.) Elizabeth worked at her hospital for more than 20 years before retiring to her hometown of Aldeburgh, where she decided to run for mayor. At the age of 72, she became the first female mayor in all of Britain, and she served two terms. (Just reading about it is exhausting!)

its original mission and became the New Hospital for Women in London, a teaching hospital staffed entirely by women. And guess who became professor of gynecology at the new hospital? Yep, Dr. Elizabeth Blackwell, who happened to be living in England at the time.

Despite her accomplishments, Elizabeth was still unsatisfied with her loophole license. So she did the logical thing—she learned French, enrolled in the more liberal Sorbonne University in Paris, and became the first woman in France to graduate with an MD. (If you thought learning biology and anatomy in your native language was hard, try doing it in a foreign language!)

Still reading Dr. Blackwell's handbook, Elizabeth came back and cofounded the London School of Medicine for Women in 1874. In 1883, she was appointed dean of the

school and oversaw its expansion. Today, the school has evolved into the Elizabeth Garrett Anderson Wing of University College London's Medical School.

At any point in her journey, Elizabeth could have hopped the pond, followed in her mentor's footsteps, and gotten her degree in America. But she felt it was her duty to bring medical education to the women of England, no matter how many disappointments she faced in the process. By the time Elizabeth was finished with Britain, she had accomplished for it everything Dr. Blackwell had done for the United States. So, as kindred spirits go, she could have done worse!

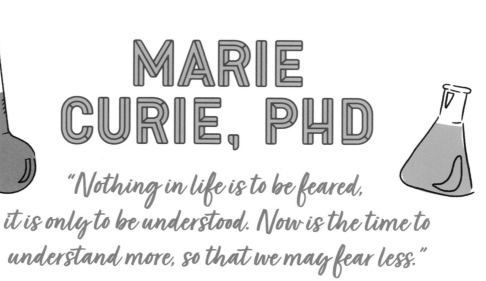

MARIE CURIE, PHD

"Nothing in life is to be feared, it is only to be understood. Now is the time to understand more, so that we may fear less."

—MARIE CURIE

★ DISCOVERED TWO NEW CHEMICAL ELEMENTS AND ADVANCED BOTH X-RAY TECHNOLOGY AND CANCER TREATMENT

★ BECAME THE FIRST WOMAN TO EARN NOBEL PRIZES IN TWO CATEGORIES AND TO EARN A PHD FROM A FRENCH UNIVERSITY

Don't let those stern, unsmiling photos of Marie Curie fool you. Sure, she may look like that scary librarian who whisper-yelled at you for typing too loudly. And yes, she was a serious, history-making scientist. But each of Marie's incredible accomplishments was the result of her childlike wonder. (It turns out that people just didn't smile in old photos. So you can't hold that against her.)

Even as a child in Poland, Maria Skłodowska approached life with boundless curiosity. Every new discovery brought her joy. (Having two teachers for parents might have had something

to do with it.) But money was tight, and a college education was just out of her reach.

Did that stop Maria? Of course not! As she herself once said, "We must have perseverance and above

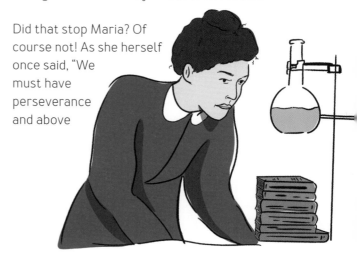

THE LITTLE CURIES

During World War I, Marie worked to develop small, mobile x-ray units that could be used to find fractures, shrapnel, and bullets in wounded soldiers near the battlefront. She toured Paris as the director of the Red Cross Radiological Service, asking for money, supplies, and vehicles to support the effort. In October 1914, the Petites Curies (or *Little Curies*) were ready for use. Marie, alongside her 17-year-old daughter Irène, saved countless lives with those mobile units.

88

Ra

Radium

226

all confidence in ourselves. We must believe that we are gifted for something and that this thing must be attained." So Maria struck a deal with her equally studious sister Bronya: she would work as a governess to support Bronya's education, and then Bronya would return the favor.

In 1891, Maria enrolled in the Sorbonne University and threw herself into the education she'd always dreamed of. She rediscovered her love for math and science (a love she inherited from her father). And by 1894, Maria had completed a master's degree in physics and another degree in mathematics.

That same year, Maria discovered another love: Pierre Curie. The two soon married and became the dynamic duo of the University of Chemistry and Physics in Paris, researching the "invisible rays" (radiation) given off by uranium. It was around that time that Maria adopted the French spelling of her name, which is how she became the now-famous Madame Marie Curie.

While working to extract uranium ore, Marie noticed something no one else had: the mineral containing the ore (called *pitchblende*) was even more radioactive than the uranium itself. Her curiosity piqued, she started to connect the dots. For one thing, she thought, there must be a third radioactive element in the pitchblende. For another, it would have to be pretty tiny for no one else to have discovered it.

Marie and Pierre worked tirelessly to uncover the culprit. They ground up the pitchblende, dissolved it in acid, and separated the different elements to reveal a black powder that was 330 times more

PAYING IT FORWARD

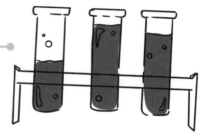

For Marie and Pierre, science was a labor of love—money and recognition were unintentional by-products. In fact, they often refused awards and sent prize money to family, friends, and scientific institutions. Marie even tried to donate her gold Nobel Prize medals to the French National Bank during the war, but they refused her. She and Pierre also chose not to patent the radium-isolation process because they wanted other scientists to have free access to it. Everything they did, they did for the benefit of others.

radioactive than uranium. In a tribute to Marie's native country, they called the element *polonium*. But a third radioactive element seemed to be lurking in the pitchblende.

Although Marie and Pierre knew this element existed, they would need a lot of pitchblende to prove it. Of course, anything containing uranium was going to be pricey. But Marie had the brilliant idea to work with a factory in Austria that extracted uranium and to buy the "useless" leftovers for cheap.

In 1902—after 4 years of grinding, dissolving, filtering, precipitating, collecting, re-dissolving, crystalizing, and re-crystalizing—Marie finally isolated the new element: radium. The discovery earned her and Pierre a share of the 1903 Nobel Prize in Physics. Around that same time, Marie added PhD to her résumé.

After Marie lost Pierre to a tragic accident, she continued his work as a professor at the Sorbonne, becoming the first female professor at the institution. She also continued with their research, eventually winning a second Nobel Prize, this time the Nobel Prize in Chemistry, in 1911, for creating a means of measuring radioactivity. After World War I, Marie continued to research, teach, and run the labs at the Sorbonne's Radium Institute as well as travel the world to give lectures and promote an international exchange of ideas for the League of Nations.

Sadly, Marie's life was cut short by the very element she had devoted it to. But she spent her life following her curiosity, shining a light into dark corners, and making an impact that she knew would outlive her. She paved the way not only for women in science, but also for the cancer treatments we use today.

YNÉS MEXÍA

"In all my travels I've never been attacked by a wild animal, lost my way or caught a disease. . . . I don't think there's any place in the world where a woman can't venture."

—YNÉS MEXÍA

★ FIRST MEXICAN–AMERICAN FEMALE BOTANIST, WITH 50 PLANT SPECIES NAMED AFTER HER

★ COLLECTED MORE THAN 145,000 PLANT SPECIMENS AND DISCOVERED TWO PLANT GENERA AND 500 PLANT SPECIES

When you think of the word "scientist," you probably imagine people in white coats staring intently at Petri dishes or holding glass tubes. But in this book alone, you can find scientists who invent new things, observe oceans, perform surgery, and explore space. That's the great thing about STEM—there's something for everyone. And, luckily for Ynés Mexía (who would have been miserable in a lab), fate had something else in mind.

The daughter of a Mexican diplomat and an American who were often at odds, Texas-born Ynés spent an unhappy childhood feeling alone and isolated. That feeling followed her into adulthood. After a difficult marriage, Ynés sought a fresh start in San Francisco, California.

Ynés decided to focus on strengthening her mental health in her new surroundings, starting with enjoying more time outdoors. She spent joyful days hiking and camping with the Sierra Club and the Save the Redwoods League. Finally, in nature, she felt at peace. With a renewed sense of purpose, she enrolled in

natural history classes at the University of California, Berkeley.

As a 51-year-old woman, Ynés got a few stares on campus. But she discovered something else about herself—she was fearless. And that fearlessness earned her a spot on a 2-month plant-collecting expedition in her father's native country, Mexico. It also resulted in her ditching the expedition and securing sponsorship for a 2-year solo trip. Ynés returned to America with more than 1,500 plant specimens, some of which had not yet been discovered by scientists.

Ynés wasn't just fearless, she was also made for science. She had an incredible memory, which kept her from collecting repeats. She'd also discovered a longing for the quiet wonder of nature. And, most surprising to the men in her field, she didn't mind a bit the slogging through bogs, climbing steep slopes, hopping between rocks, or being soaked through by rain (especially because baths were few and far between).

Traveling by any means necessary—foot or horse, car or train, canoe or steamboat—Ynés collected plants from Alaska to Tierra del Fuego at South America's southernmost tip. She even made a 3,000-mile trip through the Amazon. (People were always surprised to find a woman traveling alone, never mind dodging danger like Indiana Jones in a dress.)

Ynés loved every insane minute of her work. "I have a job where I produce something real and lasting," she said. After all, plants are essential—they

JUST A FEW BRUISES

Like most careers in the early 1900s, botany was considered too rough a pursuit for women. If you're going to go traipsing through uncharted jungle, you're bound to get a few scrapes and bruises. And, boy, did Ynés get her fair share of those. She survived earthquakes and volcanoes, poisonous berries, and even tumbling off a cliff while reaching for a plant. That last mishap resulted in some broken bones, but it didn't stop her. In fact, she later said, "After more than two years in the wilds of South America, I find myself longing for a nice, quiet jungle again." Like all pioneers of science, Ynés was great at proving the naysayers wrong.

provide not only solace and beauty but also oxygen, food, and a quarter of our medicines. In 13 years of adventures and expeditions, Ynés collected more than 145,000 plant specimens (beating the pants off all of the men in her field). Of the 500 new plant species she discovered, 50 are named after her.

After her death, many of those whose lives Ynés touched with her work wrote beautiful tributes. William E. Colby, secretary of the Sierra Club, wrote, "All who knew Ynés Mexía could not fail to be impressed by her friendly, unassuming spirit, and by that rare courage which enabled her to travel, much of the time alone, in lands where few would dare to follow." That lonely young girl had become the stuff of legends in the scientific community.

Ynés never did complete her degree, but her education was unique. The career that followed made her a household name among botanists, an inspiring presence in the history books, and a pioneering force in our understanding of the plants indigenous to our planet. And she did it all without stepping foot in a laboratory!

NEVER TOO LATE

The stories of the women in this book and the countless others who have made history are incredible, inspiring, and captivating. But they can also be a little daunting. Their passion and focus are hard to come by, especially when you're young. Rest assured, not every great woman discovered her calling in diapers. Ynés found hers by accident, at age 51, while enjoying some much-needed "me time." She had no intention of changing the world. She just really liked plants. So, if you haven't found your "thing" yet, don't worry about it! You will.

GERTRUDE CATON THOMPSON

"Archaeology is the study of humanity itself."
—MARGARET MURRAY, MENTOR TO GERTRUDE CATON THOMPSON

★ LED THE FIRST ALL FEMALE ARCHAEOLOGICAL EXPEDITION AND DEVELOPED GROUNDBREAKING EXCAVATION METHODS

★ UNCOVERED THE TRUTH ABOUT ZIMBABWE'S HERITAGE, WHICH LED TO A RENEWAL OF NATIONAL PRIDE AND THE RENAMING OF THE COUNTRY

Telling people something they don't want to hear is one of the hardest things a person can do. A woman telling a room full of angry men something they didn't want to hear in the late 1920s? That was even harder. But Gertrude Caton Thompson did it with her head held high, and that courage helped shape a grateful nation's identity.

Gertrude fell in love with archaeology on a trip to Egypt with her mom. Attending a lecture series on ancient Greece at the British Museum fanned the flames, so she spent her next vacation volunteering as a bottle washer at an excavation site in the south of France. And she couldn't wait to do more.

In 1921, Gertrude enrolled at University College London to study under a pioneer in Egyptology and a female force of nature: Margaret Murray. But it wasn't long before she found herself in Egypt again, this time at a dig in Abydos led by

Fayum Oasis

famous archaeologist Flinders Petrie. He gave Gertrude invaluable practical experience and a method of dating excavation sites that she would later use in her own expeditions.

It's no wonder, then, that Gertrude was one of Margaret Murray's star students and a shoo-in for her cave excavation in Malta with fellow archaeologist Edith Guest. Before long,

Gertrude was running her own excavations with other amazing women, like geologist Elinor Wight Gardner. The pair initiated the first archaeological survey of the Fayum Oasis in Egypt and excavated a number of sites in the region.

Three years later, Gertrude found herself in southern Africa, studying the impressive and controversial ruins of Great Zimbabwe. The ruins were in Rhodesia, a country named after British imperialist Cecil Rhodes, who had conquered it in a bloody and unnecessary war against its native people. Gertrude and her all-female excavation team had their work cut out for them—they were there to prove Cecil wrong.

White European men like Cecil Rhodes often had a bad habit of dismissing the history and culture of indigenous people. They believed people of color were inferior to them, and

LIKE HISTORY-MAKING DOMINOES

With her diligence and strength, Gertrude is an amazing role model for women in science. But equally incredible is the vast network of noteworthy women who came before her, taught her, worked with her, learned from her, and came after her. Just a couple of examples: the UK's first female archaeology lecturer, Margaret Murray, who mentored Gertrude, and celebrated archaeologist Kathleen Kenyon, whom Gertrude mentored. (Gertrude also gave famous paleoanthropologist Mary Leakey her start in the field.) Without each woman's willingness to be the first, the accomplishments of the next might not have been possible.

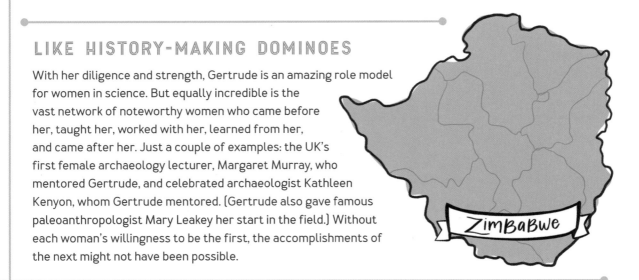

ZIMBABWE

they couldn't have little things like history and truth getting in the way of that belief. So, when German geologist Karl Mauch "discovered" the ruins in 1871 (the way that Europeans "discovered" things that already belonged to native populations), he declared that they were too remarkable to have been built by the local Shona people.

When Rhodes took power, he asked amateur archaeologist J. Theodore Bent to determine the origins of the ruins. Seeing evidence of an established civilization that traded with Chinese, Arab, and Persian cultures in the ruins, Bent declared that a northern white race must have been responsible for them. And just to make sure no one could say anything to the contrary, he appointed a journalist named Richard Hall as the site's curator and let him remove entire layers of contradictory evidence.

Only one man—archaeologist David Randall-McIver—believed the ruins were of African origin. And, using her own meticulous methods of excavation, Gertrude was able to prove him right beyond a shadow of a doubt. She presented the iron-clad evidence at a meeting of the British Association for the Advancement of Science in Johannesburg and got exactly the reaction you'd expect. The men threw fits.

Gertrude's claims caused a scandal that followed her for years, but she didn't care.

GREAT ZIMBABWE

Thanks to Gertrude (and archaeologists like her) surveying stone structures and unearthing foreign artifacts, we now know quite a bit about Great Zimbabwe. The ancient city existed between the 11th and 15th centuries and was divided into three separate sections. As the capital of the Kingdom of Zimbabwe, Great Zimbabwe was a hub in an advanced global trading network and packed in up to 18,000 people at its peak. In other words, it was a lot like the busy cities we live in and visit today.

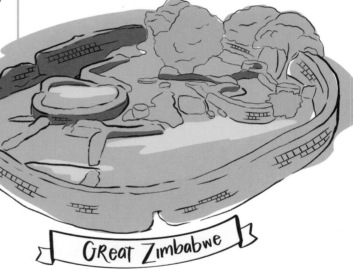

Great Zimbabwe

(Rumor has it that she kept angry letters from local experts in a file marked "insane.") The truth was the truth, and she'd go on telling it for the rest of her life. Thanks in part to Gertrude's discovery of that truth, Rhodesia eventually reclaimed its heritage and became the Zimbabwe we know today.

JANAKI AMMAL, PHD

"I am a born wanderer. There is a great restlessness in me."

—JANAKI AMMAL

★ CREATED A SWEETER SUGARCANE HYBRID THAT INDIA COULD GROW IN ITS OWN SOIL

★ ADVOCATED FOR INDIA'S BOTANICAL HERITAGE AND HELPED CREATE ONE OF THEIR LARGEST PRESERVES

As the sixteenth child born to her father in Thalassery, India, Edavaleth Kakkat Janaki Ammal could have gotten lost in the shuffle. But, thanks to her dad's own love of learning, she had the kind of education most young Indian girls at the time couldn't dream of having. She also had the kind of life many young Indian women wouldn't have dared to choose. By the end of it, Janaki would earn her doctorate, travel the world, and become a pioneer of botany and environmental preservation.

Janaki had zero interest in a traditional life. She watched her sisters enter into arranged marriages and, when it was her turn, chose education instead. First came the bachelor's degree from Queen Mary's College, Madras. Then, the honors degree in botany from Presidency College. After teaching for 3 years at the Women's Christian College in Madras, she received the opportunity of a lifetime: a scholarship to the University of Michigan.

During two separate stints at the school, Janaki earned a master's degree in science and a doctorate in botany. She was the first Indian woman ever to earn a PhD in the United States. Thanks to her focus on cytology and the breeding of hybrid plants, she then caught the attention of the Imperial Sugar

THE ROYAL TREATMENT

Janaki, like many other travelers, had to pass through Ellis Island on her way into the United States to study at the University of Michigan. The fact that she had come on a prestigious scholarship didn't stop officials from detaining her. But they didn't keep her long. She told her niece, "I think my long hair and attire in traditional Indian silks allowed me in straight away. They asked me whether I was an Indian princess. I did not deny it."

Cane Institute (now the Sugarcane Breeding Institute) in Coimbatore.

At the time, the best sugarcane had to be imported to India, which wasn't cheap and didn't give India any control over the crops. Janaki identified and crossed dozens of plants to find a hybrid that could grow in India's tropical climate and deliver consistent sweetness. In fact, it's the variety that India still grows and enjoys today.

Instead of being grateful for the extra zip in their coffee, Janaki's male colleagues snubbed her success. Their motive might have been professional jealousy or sexism. It could have also been snobbery (Janaki came from a lower-class background). But it didn't make Janaki want to stick around. She spent the next decade in England, where she found more respect but had to endure German bombings during World War II.

In 1951, Prime Minister Jawaharlal Nehru asked Janaki to come home. He recruited her to overhaul the Botanical Survey of India and help the country recover from famine. But Janaki soon realized that the government's attempts to boost food production had destroyed millions of acres of native plant life. Throughout her career, she had been focused on engineering better plants. Now, she found herself desperate to preserve the ones that already existed.

Janaki used her platform as a respected scientist and as officer on special duty at the Botanical Survey to advocate for India's indigenous plants. And she did so on an international stage. In 1955, she was the only woman to attend a symposium in Chicago called "Man's Role in Changing the Face of the Earth," where she spoke about how the mass production of cereals ravaged India's botanical history.

That environmentalist mission led to another: to save the Silent Valley forests that were about to be flooded for a hydroelectric project. Using her decades of experience and the respect they'd earned her, she organized a massive study of the Valley plants to preserve them for science. Not only did the government give up on the project, but it also declared the forest a national park.

Janaki didn't live to see her greatest triumph, but she never expected to. She told her niece, "My work is what will survive." And it has, in her hybrid magnolias, India's home-grown sugar supply, and the Silent Valley National Park. It also lives on in numerous scholarships created in her name and a beautiful hybrid rose called "E. K. Janaki Ammal" in honor of her remarkable career and contribution to plant science.

STUCK IN PRODUCTIVE LIMBO

In 1939, Janaki traveled to the United Kingdom to attend a conference and suddenly found herself stuck there because of World War II. But she took the detour in stride and made the most of it. Janaki spent 6 years at the John Innes Institute in Norfolk working closely with geneticist C. D. Darlington and coauthoring the *Chromosome Atlas of Cultivated Plants*. (The book, which features 100,000 plants, is still used by scientists today.) She then became the first salaried female staff member of the Royal Horticultural Society (RHS) and worked on cultivating bigger, faster-growing plants. The *Magnolia kobus Janaki Ammal*, a magnolia shrub she created, still blooms at the RHS's garden at Wisley every spring. So, the next time you're stuck somewhere you don't want to be, find a way to make it work for you!

KATHARINE BURR BLODGETT, PHD

"The scientist is motivated primarily by curiosity and a desire for truth."

—IRVING LANGMUIR, MENTOR TO KATHARINE BURR BLODGETT

★ INVENTED "INVISIBLE GLASS," WHICH CANCELS OUT REFLECTIONS AND IS USED IN A VARIETY OF PRODUCTS TODAY

★ SAVED COUNTLESS LIVES IN WORLD WAR II WITH HER INVENTIONS

Do you wear glasses? Use a computer? Take pictures? Ride in cars? Then you have Katharine Burr Blodgett and her work with monomolecular layers to thank. The research she did in a New York lab in 1935 not only saved lives then but also made life infinitely better for us today.

Katharine's story is like something you would see in a movie. It starts just weeks before her birth, when her father was shot and killed by a burglar in Schenectady, New York. Three years later, Katharine's mother moved the family to Europe (then back to New York, then back to Europe). Katharine was 8 years old before she started school, but she managed to graduate and enroll at Bryn Mawr College when she was just 15 years old. At 19, she discovered her life's purpose: science.

The real story behind Katharine's career in science is a little more mundane than that. Like kids all over the world, Katharine took a tour of her dad's old workplace and got offered a job. That workplace just so happened to be innovation giant General Electric, and her guide just so happened to be her dad's former colleague (and future Nobel Prize winner) Irving Langmuir. OK, maybe it's not so mundane.

Irving could tell that Katharine had a natural talent for math and science. He encouraged her to get her master's degree so that she could come back to work at GE, which she did in 1918. After 6 years of proving herself as a research scientist, Katharine knew she'd need her doctorate to move up at GE. Irving used his influence at Cambridge University to get her a spot in a coveted and male-dominated program.

In 1926, Katharine became the first woman to receive a PhD in physics from the university. Then she returned to New York to become the first female scientist to work at the GE Laboratory. And she got right back to work with Irving.

Thanks in part to his mentorship, Katharine's time at GE was filled with history-making innovation. Irving had devised a technique for creating single-molecule-thin

HELPING HANDS

One thing you might have noticed about remarkable women like Katharine is that they didn't make history alone. No one does. Irving Langmuir gave Katharine a job. Katharine inspired her niece and namesake, Katharine Blodgett Gebbie, to become an award-winning astrophysicist. Katharine Gebbie oversaw four Nobel Prize winners. And on and on it goes. Whether someone paved the way for them, taught them, mentored them, or just encouraged them, every successful person has someone to thank. Having help along the way doesn't take away from your triumphs—it makes them possible.

films of oil on water. Katharine built on that technique, layering the oil one molecule by one molecule onto glass to make it perfectly clear and non-reflective. In other words, she got rid of the glare.

She also figured out how to measure the layers, which was important because 35,000 of them were only as thick as a single piece of paper. Katharine discovered that the color of the glass changed with the layer's thickness. By creating a color gauge (kind of like a colored ruler), she could measure the molecular coatings to one millionth of an inch just by matching up the colors.

Katharine's "invisible glass" changed the way we saw movies when it was used in cameras and projectors. (People were stunned by the clarity of the first film that used it—the iconic *Gone with the Wind*.) But the glass has done more than up our entertainment game. It also saved lives when used in submarine periscopes and airplane spy cameras during World War II.

Katharine's college thesis on the chemical structure of gas masks also came in handy during the war, helping her devise safer smokescreens for the troops. And, if that wasn't enough, she invented a technique for de-icing airplane wings, too. It allowed pilots to fly in previously dangerous conditions.

Throughout her career, Katharine earned eight patents for her inventions, countless awards, and even a little press in popular magazines like *Life* and *Time*. But she preferred to let her work speak for itself. And it's still saying quite a lot! Scientists today are studying her techniques in hopes of applying them to newer tech, like microchips. And now you'll think of her every time you snap a selfie.

A BALANCED LIFE

It's easy to think that these incredible women spent every waking hour devoted to their work. But, however accomplished they were, they were also human. They had families and relationships and hobbies just like anyone else. Katharine, for example, acted in a community theater group, volunteered with various charities, wrote funny poems, and spent her summers gardening and stargazing in upstate New York. It's important to give your brain a break every now and then!

BARBARA MCCLINTOCK, PHD

"If you know you are on the right track, if you have this inner knowledge, then nobody can turn you off. . . no matter what they say."

—BARBARA MCCLINTOCK

★ THE FIRST WOMAN TO WIN AN UNSHARED NOBEL PRIZE IN PHYSIOLOGY OR MEDICINE

★ DISCOVERED "JUMPING GENES," WHICH TRANSFORMED OUR UNDERSTANDING OF GENETICS

Have you ever said something totally reasonable only to have people look at you like you have three heads? Frustrating, right? Barbara McClintock knew the feeling. She did the research, followed the evidence, and presented a scientific breakthrough to a room full of people who weren't ready to hear it. It did not go well.

But Barbara wasn't fazed—she was used to doing her own thing by that point. For a woman in the early 1900s, simply attending college was an act of rebellion. Studying science made her even more extraordinary. Barbara went on to earn not only her

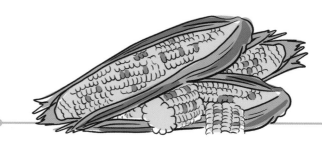

WHY CORN?

You're probably wondering, "Why corn?" This delicious crop is not only cheap and easy to grow, but it's also favored by scientists because each kernel is technically an embryo, with its own genetic makeup. That means a single ear of corn can give researchers hundreds of "offspring" to study. (Try not to think about it the next time you grab an ear at a picnic.)

bachelor's degree but also her master's and doctorate in botany at Cornell University.

During school, Barbara started researching the genetics of multicolored maize (corn). She loved working in the lab, saying once, "I was just so interested in what I was doing I could hardly wait to get up in the morning and get at it." By 1941, she had landed a full-time position at Cold Spring Harbor Laboratories in New York.

Barbara's research focused on mapping the colors and patterns on the corn. According to the known science at the time, they should have been more predictable than they were. By planting and carefully observing generation after

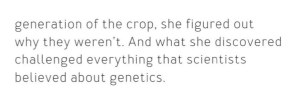

generation of the crop, she figured out why they weren't. And what she discovered challenged everything that scientists believed about genetics.

Genes, she realized, weren't locked in place. They could move around within chromosomes, resulting in an entirely different set of physical traits in the next generation. Today, these *transposable elements* are commonly called "jumping genes." Back then, they were called "impossible."

Barbara knew that the scientific community was going to have a hard time accepting this new information, so she put off publishing

GOOD INTENTIONS

If her mother had had her way, Barbara wouldn't have gone to college at all. Mrs. McClintock thought a college degree might scare off potential husbands. She meant well. After all, in 1919, getting married was often the only way for women to have financial stability. But Barbara's dad wouldn't hear of it. He made it home from the Army Medical Corps just in time to settle the dispute and see his daughter enrolled in the Cornell School of Agriculture. And between the funding from her many fellowships and her salaried positions at universities, Barbara had no problem supporting herself.

her work until other researchers confirmed it. Finally, in 1951, she stood in front of her colleagues at the Cold Spring Harbor Laboratory's annual symposium and presented the evidence. "They thought I was crazy," she said. "Absolutely mad." But Barbara didn't let it bother her.

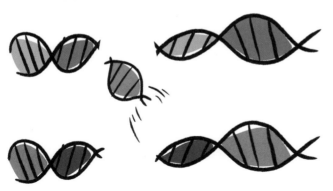

Barbara had put in the work; she knew she was right. And she enjoyed every minute she got to spend in the lab. So, instead of wasting her time seeking support from her colleagues, she just continued doing what she loved to do. Eventually, science caught up with Barbara. Thirty-two years after she presented her work, she received a Nobel Prize for it.

THE TRUTH WILL OUT

The great thing about science is that the evidence tends to speak for itself. That's why Barbara wasn't worried about the naysayers. "If you know you're right, you don't care," she said. "You know that sooner or later, it will come out in the wash." Instead of trying to convince her colleagues, she gave them the time and space to arrive at the same conclusions while she continued to do groundbreaking work.

To say that Barbara was ahead of her time is an understatement. She patiently waited more than a decade for her colleagues to catch up with her and *three* decades for the Nobel Prize that validated her insightful research. But she kept her head down, concentrated on her work, and continued to change the world with her discoveries while her peers argued about the color of corn.

So, the next time you're tempted to spend precious energy worrying about what others think, don't. Remember Barbara's story, forget about the haters, and focus on doing your best. And be gracious when you show them your shiny new Nobel medal. (Hey, you never know!)

GRACE HOPPER, PHD

"The most dangerous phrase in the language is, 'We've always done it this way.'"

—GRACE HOPPER

★ BECAME ONE OF THE FIRST COMPUTER PROGRAMMERS AND WORKED ON TOP-SECRET CALCULATIONS FOR THE NAVY DURING WORLD WAR II

★ DEVOTED HER CAREER TO CREATING SIMPLER COMPUTER LANGUAGES AND MAKING PROGRAMMING MORE ACCESSIBLE

Not all that long ago, the idea of laptops and tablets was as crazy as the idea of flying cars and teleportation. When the first computers measured 8 feet high, 3 feet deep, and 51 feet long, no one imagined that we'd use sleek little handheld computers to make phone calls. No one, except for Grace Hopper, that is.

When Grace attended Vassar College, computer science didn't exist yet. Neither did computers. Her career in STEM began with a love of mathematics. After earning her bachelor's and master's in the subject, she instilled that love in others by teaching at Vassar College. And in 1934, she became one of the few women to earn her PhD in mathematics from Yale University.

But when World War II began, Grace felt called to leave her teaching position and join the war effort. The rest, as they say, is history! As a lieutenant of the US Naval Reserve, she became not just one of the first *female* computer programmers, but one of the *first* computer programmers. The computer she programmed was that beast of a machine described above, called the Mark I.

Grace literally wrote the book on the Mark I (a 561-page programming manual that was the first of its kind in the world). And after working

IN THE RIGHT PLACE

The US military is often at the forefront of innovation, always finding new ways to keep us safe. In fact, we have the research arm of the US Defense Department to thank for the internet. And Grace was happy to be a part of that history of advancement. "Humans are allergic to change," she said. "They love to say, 'We've always done it this way.' I try to fight that. That's why I have a clock on my wall that runs counter-clockwise." Grace's irreverent methods not only fit right in, but they also helped move the Navy forward.

One of Grace's greatest accomplishments, though, was the creation of FLOW-MATIC, the first programming language to use simple word-based commands. Grace believed that creating a way to write programs in plain English could help bring more people to the emerging field. She fought for 3 years for permission to tackle the project, but her persistence paid off.

FLOW-MATIC became the basis for another well-known programming language: COBOL (short for *common business-oriented language*). Grace used her natural gift for communication to convince both the military and private companies that COBOL was the best tool for the job. And by the 1970s, the programming language was being used around the world.

Throughout her many years in the Navy and her stints in the private sector, Grace never left teaching behind. She taught at a number of colleges after Vassar, and she organized

with that 5-ton hunk of metal and vacuum tubes, she knew that computers were the future. She even said that she wished she could live until January 1, 2000, to see how they had changed the world—and to laugh at the skeptics who thought they wouldn't.

Grace devoted her life to making that vision a reality. First, she created shared libraries of code that programmers could copy and paste so they wouldn't have to retype the same code over and over. Then, she developed the first-ever compiler, which allowed programmers to use math symbols instead of a computer's binary code. (Compilers not only made writing programs much easier but also made it possible to write for multiple computers.)

MARK 1 COMPUTER

independent workshops and conferences to train and inspire new programmers. "If you ask me what accomplishment I'm most proud of," she once said, "the answer would be all the young people I've trained over the years; that's more important than writing the first compiler."

True to her Navy training, Grace always kept her eyes on the horizon. She simplified programming languages, advocated for advancements, and trained future generations of computer programmers. Everything Grace did, she did to make computers more user-friendly and to ensure their place in the future.

A BUG IN THE SYSTEM

Ever hear someone say, "There's a bug in the system"? We have Grace to thank for that turn of phrase. Although the term "bug" had been used by engineers in reference to mechanical malfunctions since the 19th century, Grace was the first to use it in reference to computers. And there's a good reason for that. When the Mark II was acting up, she discovered a literal bug in its system—a large, dead moth, to be exact. So, from that day on, that became the go-to phrase for computer glitches. Today, "debugging" is a common part of computer programming.

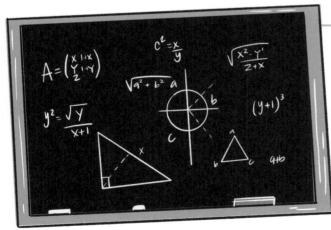

Grace's legacy lives on not only in the computers we use every day, but also in the new generations being trained to program them. You'll find her name on training programs, scholarships, and competitions devoted to making computer science more accessible to women and girls. Through them, Grace continues to create the future of computing she imagined.

RACHEL CARSON

"Those who dwell among the beauties and mysteries of the Earth are never alone or weary of life."

—RACHEL CARSON

★ AUTHOR OF *SILENT SPRING*, A BOOK THAT LAUNCHED AN ENVIRONMENTAL MOVEMENT AND A NUMBER OF GOVERNMENT POLICIES

★ TRANSLATED COMPLEX SCIENTIFIC RESEARCH INTO CAPTIVATING PROSE THAT GAVE READERS A FULLER UNDERSTANDING OF THE WORLD AROUND THEM

Have you ever wondered why the sky is blue? Or how birds know exactly where to go each winter? Or which creatures have yet to be discovered in the deepest reaches of the ocean? If so, you might have a bit of scientist in you. But if you haven't, you're not alone. Plenty of people can appreciate a blue sky without wondering why it exists.

And those who do wonder might not make it through the explanation (which has to do with gases and particles and wavelengths and light). In fact, one of the biggest obstacles for scientists is translating their work into something that everyone can understand. It's not easy. Not every scientist is a natural communicator, and not every writer or speaker has a mind for science. But when it's a matter of life or death, you really need someone who can do both.

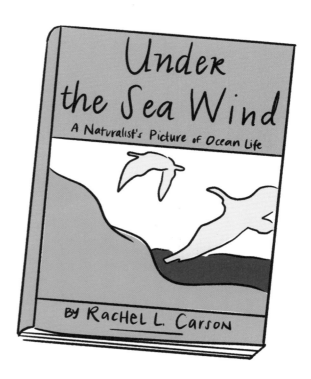

Rachel Carson was one of those rare, brilliant people. Her ability to both understand the interconnectedness of the natural world *and* get people to care about it is unmatched. And it's why she was able to create such monumental changes in public policy and public opinion.

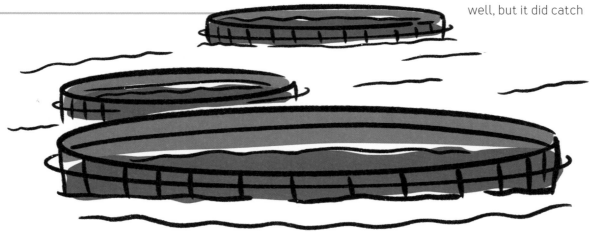

THE POWER OF PASSION

Objectivity is great, but there's nothing like passion to get your point across. Rachel never thought twice about rolling up her sleeves (and pant legs) and getting dirty. She was fearless—climbing rocks, wading into tide pools, and even exploring late at night with nothing but a flashlight. She understood how things worked under the sea because she got up close and personal with its inhabitants. And by describing them with all of the wonder she felt, she was able to act as a living, breathing connection between her readers and a world they might never see.

Rachel didn't plan on a career in biology. As a student at the Pennsylvania College for Women (now Chatham College), she had her heart set on becoming a writer. But she couldn't fight her farmgirl roots. Exploring the orchards, fields, forests, and streams near her Pennsylvania home had left her with a deep love of nature and a desire to know more about it. So, like a lot of college students, she switched her major.

Lucky for her, Rachel found a part-time job that spoke to both of her talents: writing 7-minute radio programs on marine life for the US Bureau of Fisheries. But she never stopped aiming higher. The more Rachel learned, the more articles she submitted to newspapers and magazines. She needed people to understand that their actions were having an impact on the natural world—and it wasn't good.

While moving up in the Bureau (and becoming one of only two women at the professional level there), Rachel wrote her first book, *Under the Sea Wind*. It didn't sell well, but it did catch

Pennsylvania

the attention of the newly created US Fish and Wildlife Service. Rachel went from being an aquatic biologist to assistant editor and then editor-in-chief of all of the department's publications. Still, she knew she was meant for bigger things.

In 1951, 10 years after publishing her first book, Rachel published her first best seller: *The Sea Around Us*. Its success brought her the financial freedom to leave her job, buy a house in Maine, and write her next best

THE SWELLING OF SEAS

Before Rachel discovered that she wouldn't live long enough to write another book, she already had the subject for one in mind: climate change. She wrote, "We live in an age of rising seas. In our own lifetime we are witnessing a startling alteration of climate." That was in the late 1950s. More than half a century later, climate change has become an immediate concern. We see its impact almost daily in catastrophic storms and vanishing species. We'll never get to read the world-changing book Rachel surely would have written, but we can take up her cause and help protect our planet.

seller, *The Edge of the Sea*, in 1955. This book introduced readers to the idea of *ecosystems* (where living organisms and their environment support each other).

Rachel's next book brought the concept of ecosystem connection onto dry land. In *Silent Spring*, her most impactful work, Rachel tackled the deadly effects of pesticides. She turned years of scientific study into, as her editor put it, "literature, full of beauty and loveliness and depth of feeling." By following the poison through the food chain, Rachel helped her readers understand its true dangers. Pests, wildlife, plants, *and people* were dying.

Unfortunately, so was Rachel. While fighting (and winning) a war against the chemical industry, she was losing a battle with cancer. But she never let that stop her from writing and advocating for *Silent Spring*. Her work led to a governmental review of pesticide policy, the banning of the toxic pesticide DDT, the rise of environmental activism, and the creation of the Environmental Protection Agency. By sharing her passion with the world, Rachel Carson changed it.

DOROTHY CROWFOOT HODGKIN, PHD

"I was captured for life by chemistry and crystals."

—DOROTHY CROWFOOT HODGKIN

★ DISCOVERED THE ATOMIC STRUCTURE OF PENICILLIN, VITAMIN B12, AND INSULIN—ALL IMPORTANT BREAKTHROUGHS FOR MEDICAL TREATMENTS

★ AWARDED THE 1964 NOBEL PRIZE IN CHEMISTRY

Following your dreams can lead to amazing breakthroughs, but so can simply following your curiosity. Groundbreaking scientists like Dorothy Crowfoot Hodgkin are proof of that. They notice something small and, instead of letting their interest float by unexplored, they follow it. Every step they take stokes a fire they didn't know had been lit inside of them. And before they know it, a full-blown passion emerges. That's the stuff dreams are made of.

Dorothy's dream of contributing to lifesaving medical treatments certainly didn't start out that big and showy. Her years of scientific study can be traced back to playing with chemistry and crystals as a little girl. With the encouragement of family and family friends, that pastime became a passion. Dorothy became one of two girls to earn special permission to study chemistry with the boys' class. (This was in 1921, when the only sciences taught to girls involved cooking and cleaning.) And she knew then that she wanted to know more.

On her 16th birthday, Dorothy received a copy of Nobel Prize winner William Henry Bragg's book about X-ray crystallography, and she was hooked. This cutting-edge method allowed scientists to see the structure of molecules, which make up, well, pretty much everything! And knowing how the molecules are put together helps us understand how they work, *and* how we can use them to our advantage.

A FORCE FOR GOOD

Aside from her 35-year-long mission to solve the structure of insulin, Dorothy dedicated her life to promoting world peace. She had lived through the loss of four uncles in World War I. She also had a deep sense of empathy and social justice that was instilled in her by her mother. So she became active in the League of Nations and Science for Peace. She also served as president of the Pugwash Conference for 12 years, resigning only after seeing a global ban on nuclear weapons put in place. Whether she was working in the lab or speaking at a conference, Dorothy was always focused on making the world a better place.

Dorothy was entranced. She spent the next several years studying chemistry and working with X-ray crystallography at Somerville College (University of Oxford) and Newnham College (at University of Cambridge). While earning her PhD, she discovered her life's work: studying the structures of proteins.

Proteins are the most important molecules in our body—they have an impact on everything the body does. And in 1932, no one understood them. When Dorothy and

her mentor, John Desmond Bernal, first used X-ray crystallography to analyze pepsin (a digestive enzyme that breaks down proteins), they realized how much they could learn about proteins with the technology.

Dorothy decided to shoot for the moon and to tackle insulin, a protein that's incredibly important in the treatment of diabetes. But insulin was pretty big, even as proteins go, and the technology of the time couldn't do what Dorothy needed it to do. She wasn't discouraged, though. She

simply started again with smaller molecules and worked her way up.

First up was penicillin. Although it's common now, penicillin was a brand-new miracle treatment for infections in the early 1940s. But knowing that penicillin worked as an antibiotic wasn't the same as knowing *how* it worked. By solving penicillin's structure in 1946, Dorothy gave scientists the information they needed to create even more effective medications. We have our pick of amazing antibiotics today because of her.

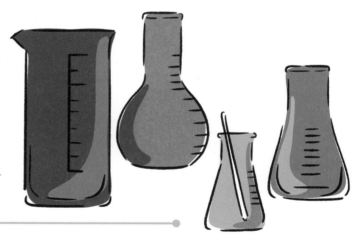

Next, Dorothy tackled the incredibly complex vitamin B12, which is essential to every single cell of the human body. Scientists had been trying for years to figure out the vitamin's structure, and Dorothy knew that X-ray crystallography was the key. She solved the structure of B12 in 1955 (which led to a better understanding of the disease known as pernicious anemia) and was awarded the Nobel Prize in Chemistry in 1964.

Through it all, Dorothy continued to work on solving the structure of insulin. It took her 35 years. But she never gave up, even fighting through the crippling pain of rheumatoid arthritis. Dorothy's work on insulin gave us the ability to treat the more than 400 million people affected by diabetes today.

When Dorothy started playing with crystals as a child, she never could have known her work would save millions of lives by helping doctors treat anemia, diabetes, and infection. She just followed her curiosity. So make sure you take the time to notice what makes you curious. You never know where that wonder can lead!

GREATNESS INSPIRES GREATNESS

Who inspires you? That's usually a pretty easy question to answer—we all have someone we look up to. They can be dead or alive, famous or family. It's entirely up to you! For Dorothy, it was her mom, Molly, medical missionary Mary Slessor, and her college principal Margery Fry. They inspired her so she could inspire others, like her student Margaret Roberts, who would become England's formidable Prime Minister Margaret Thatcher. Despite their political differences, the prime m inister was so inspired by Dorothy that she hung a picture of her on her office wall at Downing Street.

CHIEN-SHIUNG WU, PHD, SCD

"It is the courage to doubt what has long been believed and the incessant search for verification and proof that pushes the wheels of science forward."

—CHIEN-SHIUNG WU

★ CALLED THE "FIRST LADY OF PHYSICS," SHE DISPROVED AN ACCEPTED NATURAL LAW AND CONTRIBUTED TO THE MANHATTAN PROJECT

★ BECAME THE FIRST FEMALE INSTRUCTOR IN PRINCETON'S PHYSICS DEPARTMENT AND THE FIRST TENURED FEMALE PROFESSOR IN COLUMBIA'S PHYSICS DEPARTMENT

You might call Chien-Shiung Wu a puzzle master. She made a career out of finding the missing pieces for brilliant but baffled scientists and saving their experiments. You could also call her "the First Lady of Physics," "Queen of Nuclear Research," and "the Chinese Madame Curie"—others have. But the name her parents gave her might be the most fitting of all for a Chinese-American woman who accomplished so much; it means *Courageous Hero.*

Chien-Shiung was born to parents who believed in educating girls when most girls were taught only to make good wives. Just a year before her

Princeton University

birth, the Xinhai Revolution had overthrown the last Chinese dynasty and created the new Republic of China. And one of the revolution's leaders was Chien-Shiung's own father, Zhongyi Wu.

Zhongyi Wu founded the region's first school for girls so his daughter and others like her would have a chance at the formal education he knew they deserved. Chien-Shiung's mom, Fan Fuhua, stood by his side and persuaded families to enroll their girls. And because of them, Chien-Shiung was able to attend boarding school, a prestigious Chinese university, and some of the finest academic institutions in America.

Chien-Shiung didn't plan to spend the rest of her life in the United States. Without access to graduate schools in China, and with plans to attend the University of Michigan, she was forced to travel (by boat!) to the California coast. But she never made it to the Wolverine State. A pitstop at the University of California, Berkeley—a school at the forefront of physics research—changed her life.

Within days, she had decided to stay in California and study under the brilliant Ernest Lawrence. (It didn't hurt that she had met her future husband, Luke Yuan, during her visit.) She stayed at Berkeley for 2 years after completing her PhD before moving with Luke to the East Coast. He taught at Princeton University while she taught at Smith College, 200 miles away.

A FAMILY TRAIT

With parents like hers, it's no wonder Chien-Shiung became an outspoken advocate for women and girls in STEM. She spent much of her retirement traveling and lecturing about excelling in a male-dominated field. And she had no patience for sexism in science, saying at a 1964 MIT symposium on equality, "I wonder whether the tiny atoms and nuclei, or the mathematical symbols, or the DNA molecules have any preference for either masculine or feminine treatment." In other words, discovery doesn't care who you are. Her indomitable spirit, as much as her work, has inspired countless women to follow in her physics-loving footsteps.

A BIG ADJUSTMENT

Chien-Shiung's work ethic was the stuff of legends, but she may have had multiple reasons for spending so much time in the lab. Adjusting to life in the United States and the notoriously tricky English language wasn't easy. And, as any of us would, she missed her family, her home, and China's customs and food. But she remembered something her father told her before she went off to boarding school: "Ignore the obstacles. Just put your head down and keep walking forward." Chien-Shiung threw herself wholeheartedly into her work, with some amazing results. And she found ways to keep some of her treasured customs, including wearing traditional qipao dresses under her lab coats.

CHINA

It wasn't long before the distance and the lack of lab time at Smith got to Chien-Shiung, who vented to her former professor. His letters of recommendation earned her offers from eight esteemed universities, three of which didn't even offer degrees to women. She chose Princeton, and she became their first female professor. But just a few months later, she was recruited for the Manhattan Project (a secret government operation to develop the first nuclear weapons during World War II).

In the years that followed, puzzle-master Chien-Shiung stepped in to fix several failing experiments. She helped Enrico Fermi confirm his theory of beta decay by pointing out a flaw in his testing methods. Then, she designed an experiment for physicists Tsung-Dao Lee and Chen Ning Yang to help them test a theory called the *conservation of parity*. This theory stated that nature didn't differentiate between left and right—that reactions would always be equal in both directions. And although it was considered a set-in-stone natural *law*, Chien-Shiung's experiment proved that it wasn't true.

The discovery made national headlines, and Chien-Shiung's male colleagues won the 1957 Nobel Prize in Physics for it. She did not. She did, however, win plenty of other impressive awards and honors for her unmatched expertise, her contributions to science, and her history-making position as an inspiration to female scientists everywhere.

HEDY LAMARR

"All creative people want to do the unexpected."

—HEDY LAMARR

★ AN ACCOMPLISHED ACTOR, SHE WAS CONSIDERED "THE MOST BEAUTIFUL WOMAN IN THE WORLD" DURING HOLLYWOOD'S GOLDEN AGE OF FILM

★ IN BETWEEN MOVIES, SHE INVENTED SPREAD-SPECTRUM TECHNOLOGY, WHICH LAID THE GROUNDWORK FOR GPS, BLUETOOTH, AND WI-FI

What are you known for? The answer to that could depend on who you're with, where you are, what time of day it is, and whether you've had breakfast, right? (If someone only sees you when you're hungry, they might think you're a pretty cranky person.) No human being is just one thing. And we usually only show particular parts of ourselves to particular people. But imagine what we could do if we embraced all of the pieces of ourselves.

Ask someone what they know about Hedy Lamarr, and they'll probably tell you that she was a famous actress. And she was. But she was also a domestic abuse survivor, a brilliant inventor, a talented painter, and a feminist who started her own production company. Only now, decades after her death, are we really getting to know her. And she's definitely someone you want to know!

Hedy was born Hedwig Eva Maria Kiesler in Austria to Jewish parents. But at 19 years old, she found herself married to a man who manufactured weapons for the Nazis. To Fritz Mandl, Hedy was a possession—one he wanted all to himself. He forced her to spend her time playing hostess to his associates rather than acting in the plays and movies that she loved.

A MIND FOR MACHINERY

Hedy got her curiosity from her dad, who encouraged her to look at the world from a different perspective. He took her for long walks and helped her notice how things were made. By the time Hedy was 5 years old, she was already disassembling and reassembling her music box just to see how it worked. When she got older, she applied that mechanical mind to aviation, helping record-setting pilot Howard Hughes create faster-flying planes. Noticing that the wings on Howard's planes were too square, Hedy designed better ones by studying the fastest birds and fish. Howard called her a genius. He was one of the few people who saw what Hedy was truly capable of.

While playing hostess, Hedy listened intently to conversations about how to foil the American military. She discovered that Fritz's friends wanted to develop detection devices to listen to and jam the signals that American aircraft and weapons used to communicate with each other. Her mind whirred with the information.

By 1937, Hedy couldn't take any more. She fled to London by bicycle in the middle of the night with nothing but her jewelry, which she'd sewn into the lining of her disguise. And, as World War II loomed closer, she immigrated to the United States. It was on the ship from London to New York that she convinced Hollywood icon Louis B. Mayer to hire her at quadruple the price he'd initially offered. Hedy barely spoke English at the time, but that didn't stop her from having the kind of movie career actors dream of.

This was the "Golden Age" of Hollywood, when movies were filled with charismatic leading men like Cary Grant and Clark Gable and extraordinary women like Grace Kelly and Rosalind Russell. Hedy Lamarr had quickly become one of the fan favorites, even being dubbed "the most beautiful woman in the world." But she had much more to offer than Hollywood glamour.

Hedy spent most of her spare time tinkering at her workspace, engineering solutions to problems she'd spotted. She saw inventing as a way to fix the world's failings. But she knew that she had a part to play in life just as in her movies—the beautiful idiot. So, for the sake of her career, she kept the genius-inventor part of her hidden away, showing it to only a handful of like-minded people.

One of the lucky few was composer George Antheil, who collaborated on Hedy's greatest invention: spread-spectrum technology. This technology was Hedy's response to the Nazi plots she'd heard discussed back in Austria and an expression of her strong desire to contribute to the war effort. She realized that, by using frequency-hopping radio signals, the military could foil any attempts by the Germans to detect or jam their weapons systems.

Hedy and George patented the technology and presented it to the US Navy, which promptly turned it down. The invention was remarkable, but it was ahead of its time. The Navy eventually did adopt the technology, but Hedy never received credit or compensation for her work. Today, her frequency-hopping technology is worth $30 billion, having laid the foundation for GPS, Bluetooth, and Wi-Fi. Clearly, Hedy Lamarr was much more than just a pretty face.

AN INSPIRING IMAGE

You might be wondering why Hedy looks familiar, especially if you've never seen one of her movies. Today, Hedy's curious mind and world-changing innovation serve as inspiration for women and girls in STEM. But in her heyday, she was only known for her acting roles and otherworldly beauty, which inspired Disney's depiction of Snow White and DC Comics' Catwoman. The next time you stream the seven dwarves, remember to thank Hedy for both the movie and the Wi-Fi you use to watch it!

GERTRUDE B. ELION, PHD, SCD

"Don't be afraid of hard work. Nothing worthwhile comes easily. Don't let others discourage you or tell you that you can't do it."

—GERTRUDE B. ELION

★ DEVELOPED DRUGS TO TREAT LEUKEMIA, INFECTIONS, MALARIA, GOUT, HERPES, AND AIDS AND TO PREVENT KIDNEY TRANSPLANT REJECTION

★ SHARED THE 1988 NOBEL PRIZE IN CHEMISTRY FOR HER REVOLUTIONARY METHOD OF PRODUCING PHARMACEUTICALS

When the odds are stacked against you, you have two choices: give up or try to beat the odds. Gertrude Belle Elion chose option number 2. And she didn't just try—she beat the odds over and over again. From getting her degrees during the Great Depression, to finding work as a female chemist, and finally revolutionizing the pharmaceutical industry, Gertrude never let a slim chance stand in her way.

In the 1930s, choosing any career outside of teaching was a radical act for a woman without means. To choose chemistry was to fly in the face of common sense. Luckily, Gertrude didn't know that. It never occurred to her that women didn't work in laboratory sciences. "I saw no reason why we couldn't," she said. And she didn't give a second thought to the fact that she was the only woman in her graduate class. Gertrude focused instead on her love of the subject.

IT'S PERSONAL

Gertrude was one of those lucky people who loved school. Learning came easily to her, and she enjoyed every subject. That made it pretty hard to pick a major in college. But the loss of her grandfather changed everything. "I had no specific bent toward science until my grandfather died of stomach cancer. I decided then that nobody should suffer that much." She decided on a career in chemistry and a life devoted to finding a treatment for cancer. When her fiancé died from inflammation of his heart, Gertrude became even more devoted to her career. Just 2 years later, she saw medical advancements that would have prevented his death. She couldn't save the men she loved, but her work saved many more.

When she needed a job, though, Gertrude hit a wall. No laboratory would hire a female chemist. "I hadn't been aware that any doors were closed to me until I started knocking on them," she said. The closest she came to working in a lab was volunteering as a dishwasher in one. By the time she left the job a year and a half later, she was earning a whole $20 per week.

With the start of World War II, new possibilities opened up for women in every field. Many of the men had left their jobs to enlist or contribute to the war effort in some other way, leaving gaping holes that needed to be filled. Suddenly, Gertrude had her pick of several labs.

After a few false starts in quality control, Gertrude eventually found her way to pharmaceutical company Burroughs-Wellcome (now GlaxoSmithKline). She would spend the rest of her career there, working side by side with Dr. George H. Hitchings. Luckily for Gertrude, George appreciated her love of learning and was quite happy to pile on new and exciting responsibilities.

Together, the pair developed a new method of researching medical treatments. Pharmaceutical research usually relied on good old trial and error. Gertrude and George figured out that they could block a virus or disease from spreading by studying the differences between normal cells and affected cells. Their first success stopped leukemia in its tracks.

But Gertrude wanted to do more. Seeing that chemotherapy treatments for leukemia often led to terrible side effects, she set out to create an alternative. She discovered a less toxic compound that, when combined with other drugs, becomes an even more effective treatment for the disease. Doctors still use this treatment method today to help cure 80% of childhood leukemia.

THE RIGHT PATH

Once Gertrude decided to study chemistry, her path seemed clear: bachelor's, master's, and then doctorate. But life had other plans. Gertrude's father had lost everything in the stock market crash of 1929, just a few short years before she'd need to pay tuition. Luckily, Hunter College was a free public college. But Gertrude's master's degree would have to wait. Job opportunities were scarce during the Great Depression, so she took what she could. After a couple of years, Gertrude had saved enough money to attend graduate school part time while continuing to work odd jobs. She was prepared to do the same to earn her doctorate in chemistry, but Brooklyn Polytechnic forced her to choose a full-time path: work or PhD. Gertrude followed her gut and chose work. Years later, her success in the field proved her gut right. Gertrude received honorary PhDs from Brown University, George Washington University, and the University of Michigan, and an honorary SCD from Harvard.

Over the course of their decades-long partnership, Gertrude and George were able to design treatments for malaria, gout, herpes, AIDS, and more, securing them the Nobel Prize in 1988. But that was never Gertrude's goal. "The Nobel Prize is fine," she said, "but the drugs I've developed are rewards in themselves." Gertrude developed 45 patents and saw countless people healed, all because she refused to acknowledge the odds.

KATHERINE JOHNSON

"Some things will drop out of the public eye and will go away, but there will always be science, engineering, and technology. And there will always, always be mathematics."

—KATHERINE JOHNSON

★ CALCULATED THE FLIGHT PATH FOR ALAN SHEPHERD, THE FIRST AMERICAN TO REACH SPACE, AND FOR JOHN GLENN'S ORBITAL MISSION

★ WAS AN INTEGRAL PART OF THE MISSION TO LAND A MAN ON THE MOON IN 1969, WITH HER CALCULATIONS ENSURING THE ASTRONAUTS' SAFE RETURN

Katherine Johnson was born in West Virginia at a time when movies were silent, women couldn't vote, toasters were a new invention, and you started your car by cranking a handle. But she lived long enough to stream movies on a plane, see the invention of self-driving cars, and watch a woman run for president. And during that extraordinary lifetime, she not only saw men land on the moon, but she also helped put them there.

For Katherine, the constant in her long life was STEM. "Everything is physics and math," she said. As a child, she counted everything, from the stairs she climbed to the forks she washed. After graduating from college at the age of 18, she took the math degree she'd earned and started teaching math. And when she discovered that the National Advisory Committee for Aeronautics (the precursor to NASA) was hiring Black mathematicians (called *computers*), she jumped at the opportunity.

MORE THAN FATE

Katherine enjoyed a lifelong love of learning, which she said was "an art and a science" in and of itself. But getting the education she craved wasn't always easy. As a young Black girl in the South, she didn't have the opportunities offered to white children. Her hometown didn't even offer public school for Black children beyond eighth grade. So, what's a math prodigy to do? She didn't have to wonder, because her parents made the extraordinary choice to move their family to a better district 120 miles away.

Katherine honored her parents' sacrifice by graduating from high school at just 14 years old and attending West Virginia State College, where she found a mentor in professor W. W. Schieffelin Claytor. He encouraged Katherine to become a research mathematician, even creating a geometry class just for her. Katherine's passion for geometry was crucial to her ability to plot flight paths. So, fate might have been on Katherine's side, but it got a helping hand from a few of her favorite people.

Going from lesson plans to flight plans couldn't have been easy, but Katherine excelled at her new job. She spent 4 years at the Langley laboratory analyzing flight data and trying to figure out why certain planes had crashed. Through meticulous work, she learned that larger planes left a wake of disturbed air behind them for up to half an hour, and that could send smaller planes spiraling. By helping engineers avoid the problem, she had made air travel safer.

Katherine's next endeavor would be making space travel safer. No big deal, right? But at that time, America had yet to launch a man into space. "Everything was so new," she said.

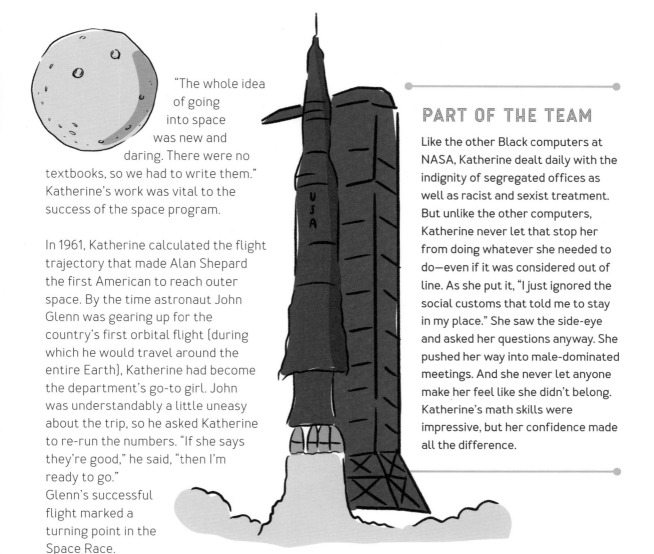

"The whole idea of going into space was new and daring. There were no textbooks, so we had to write them." Katherine's work was vital to the success of the space program.

In 1961, Katherine calculated the flight trajectory that made Alan Shepard the first American to reach outer space. By the time astronaut John Glenn was gearing up for the country's first orbital flight (during which he would travel around the entire Earth), Katherine had become the department's go-to girl. John was understandably a little uneasy about the trip, so he asked Katherine to re-run the numbers. "If she says they're good," he said, "then I'm ready to go." Glenn's successful flight marked a turning point in the Space Race.

PART OF THE TEAM

Like the other Black computers at NASA, Katherine dealt daily with the indignity of segregated offices as well as racist and sexist treatment. But unlike the other computers, Katherine never let that stop her from doing whatever she needed to do—even if it was considered out of line. As she put it, "I just ignored the social customs that told me to stay in my place." She saw the side-eye and asked her questions anyway. She pushed her way into male-dominated meetings. And she never let anyone make her feel like she didn't belong. Katherine's math skills were impressive, but her confidence made all the difference.

Katherine would say that her greatest achievement was contributing to the moon landing. After all, her calculations helped the astronauts of *Apollo 11* and *Apollo 13* return safely home. But greater still might be her influence on new generations of girls interested in STEM. She not only led by example but also actively encouraged girls to follow in her history-making footsteps.

In 2015, Katherine was honored at an event where she received the Presidential Medal of Freedom. Barack Obama said it best at the ceremony: "In her 33 years at NASA, Katherine was a pioneer who broke the barriers of race and gender, showing generations of young people that everyone can excel in math and science, and reach for the stars."

JANE COOKE WRIGHT, MD

"There's lots of fun in exploring the unknown. There's no greater thrill than in having an experiment turn out in such a way that you make a positive contribution."

—JANE COOKE WRIGHT

★ DEVELOPED CANCER TREATMENTS STILL IN USE TODAY AND PIONEERED PERSONALIZED MEDICINE

★ BECAME THE HIGHEST RANKED BLACK WOMAN AT A NATIONALLY RECOGNIZED MEDICAL INSTITUTION AND THE FIRST FEMALE PRESIDENT OF THE NEW YORK CANCER SOCIETY

Do you know the first step to changing the world? Believing you can change it. Mindset is everything. Sure, it's easy to see obstacles and feel defeated before you've even begun. But if you train yourself to see challenges instead, you'll know that you can rise to meet them.

That's how Jane Cooke Wright lived her life—seeing challenges where others saw obstacles. According to her daughter, "She never let anything stand in the way of her doing what she wanted to do." And as a woman of color in medicine in the 1960s, Jane definitely had an uphill battle ahead of her. She had to work twice as hard as men, but she never let racism or sexism stop her. She used her determination and passion for science to make breakthroughs the world had never seen, like unlocking cancer treatments.

In the 1940s, chemotherapy (the use of chemicals to kill cancer cells) was seen as a last resort. It was new and experimental, and doctors had yet to figure out the best ways to use it. Surgery was considered the best treatment option. But cutting out the cancer didn't always solve the fundamental problem with the disease: cancer cells grow uncontrollably. Plus, surgery only worked with tumors. You couldn't take a scalpel to blood cancers like leukemia, lymphoma, and myeloma.

Jane pioneered a method of delivering chemotherapeutic drugs directly to hard-to-reach tumors by injecting them into a patient's bloodstream. She also developed use of a drug that could starve cancer cells of the folic acid they needed to grow and reproduce. To this day, we still use that drug—methotrexate—to treat breast cancer, leukemia, lung cancer, osteosarcoma, and more.

When Jane took over for her father as head of the Cancer Research Foundation at Harlem Hospital in 1955, she turned her attention to personalized medicine. Never before had doctors been able to tailor their cancer treatment protocols to both the patient and the patient's particular type of cancer. By removing a piece of cancerous tissue from a patient and testing treatments against it, Jane discovered she could do just that.

But for Jane's research to do the most good, she'd have to tackle one more challenge: getting the word out about it. Lack of communication between researchers, hospitals, and medical schools was a serious problem. And Jane wasn't

GOOD GENES

It's no wonder that Jane went into medicine—her family was full of groundbreaking physicians. Her grandfather, Dr. Ceah Ketcham Wright, was born into slavery but went on to earn his medical degree after the Civil War. Her step-grandfather, Dr. William Fletcher Penn, was the first Black man to graduate from Yale Medical College. And her father, Dr. Louis T. Wright, was one of the first Black graduates of Harvard Medical School. Instead of being intimated by that incredible legacy, both Jane and her sister became trailblazing doctors themselves. Jane would even end up running the prominent cancer research center her father founded.

SHARING IS CARING

Knowledge is like pie—it's best when shared. And that's especially true when it comes to scientific knowledge. That's why, in addition to ensuring that her cancer treatments made it into hospitals around the country, Jane also shared her work with the world. She regularly traveled with oncologists to China, the former Soviet Union, Africa, and Eastern Europe to treat cancer patients. By sharing her discoveries, she saved countless lives. So, the next time you're tempted to keep quiet about something—whether you're afraid of being wrong or waiting for things to be perfect—speak up. Jane's innovative research couldn't have done anyone any good if it had stayed in the lab. And your brilliant ideas can't do anyone any good if they stay in your head!

National Cancer Advisory Board and was named professor of surgery, head of the Cancer Chemotherapy Department, and associate dean at the New York Medical College. That last position made her the highest-ranking Black woman among all medical institutions at the time.

Jane's tireless work as both a researcher and a leader in her field revolutionized the way we treat cancer today, saving millions of lives. Although she found the work fascinating, Jane's main source of motivation was the patients who would benefit from her work. Keeping them in mind helped her overcome many of the challenges she faced.

the only one who'd noticed. Together with six other oncologists (all of whom were white men), she founded the American Society of Clinical Oncology (ASCO) in 1964. This organization would help educate doctors, provide grants for training and research, and create a higher standard of care across the country.

The 1960s were busy for Jane. In addition to founding the ASCO, she served on the

NEW YORK MEDICAL COLLEGE

MARIE M. DALY, PHD

"Successful people are those who failed and kept going."

—MARIE M. DALY

★ HELPED UNCOVER THE LINK BETWEEN DIET AND HEART HEALTH, SAVING COUNTLESS PEOPLE FROM HEART ATTACKS

★ THE FIRST BLACK AMERICAN WOMAN TO EARN A PHD IN CHEMISTRY, SHE DEVOTED HER LIFE TO LIFTING UP OTHER PEOPLE OF COLOR

You know those "heart healthy" labels on everything from frozen meals to cereal boxes and pancake mix? Dr. Marie Maynard Daly is the reason those exist. Well, kind of.

Marie is actually the brilliant scientist who first connected the dots between diet and heart health. Before her groundbreaking work in the 1950s, we had no idea that the high cholesterol found in certain foods could lead to clogged arteries and heart attacks. And now that we know, we're shouting it from rooftops and butter tubs everywhere.

Marie didn't figure this out overnight, though. She had to work her way through three college degrees, multiple fellowships, several jobs, and years of research before making her discovery. And she did it all as a Black woman at a time when women and people of color were all but shunned from jobs in science.

Marie's talent and tenacity probably came from her parents. Although they didn't have access to formal education, they were lifelong learners who believed wholeheartedly that their children should receive an education. Marie's dad was a chemist at heart, and her

HER FATHER'S DAUGHTER

Marie's dad, an immigrant from the British West Indies, always wanted to be a chemist. Financial hardship forced him to drop out of Cornell University, but as a Black man, he was always going to have a hard time achieving his dream. Job opportunities in science were few and far between for minorities. But Marie was her father's daughter, and she picked up right where he left off. She never forgot the sacrifice he had to make and the struggle she, herself, faced in pursuing their dream. Marie spent her career fighting for the inclusion of women and people of color in science. In 1988, she established a scholarship at Queens College in honor of her father for minority students who wanted to study science.

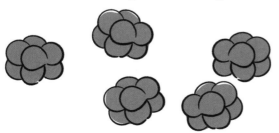

mom passed down a passion for reading. Both noticed and nurtured their daughter's gift for science.

So did her teachers at science-centered Hunter College High School, who encouraged Marie to pursue chemistry at the college level. But money was as tight for her as it had been for her father. By staying close to home and studying at Queens College, she was just able to make it. Finding the funds for graduate

school in 1942, though, meant earning a fellowship *and* working as a lab assistant. She still managed to earn her master's degree in just 1 year.

Then, almost by accident, Marie became the first Black American woman to receive a PhD in chemistry. In the 1940s, only 2% of Black American women held college degrees, let alone doctorates. But Marie felt that going to grad school was a safer choice than trying to find a job in a world where her sex and her skin color put her at a drastic disadvantage. She received her degree in chemistry in 1947 after finishing an accelerated 3-year program. At the time, she had no idea she was the first to do it.

Having studied biochemistry under an inspiring teacher, Marie found herself fascinated by how the body's chemicals help digest food. A grant from the American Cancer Society led to her landing a 7-year research program and studying how proteins are constructed in cells. Marie's work with histones (proteins that give structure to DNA) was cutting-edge at the time and laid the foundation for our understanding of cell biology today.

But it was Marie's work with Dr. Quentin B. Deming that made the biggest splash. By studying the effects of cholesterol, sugar, and other nutrients on the body, Marie was the

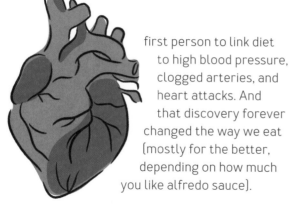

first person to link diet to high blood pressure, clogged arteries, and heart attacks. And that discovery forever changed the way we eat (mostly for the better, depending on how much you like alfredo sauce).

Over the years, Marie never lost sight of the importance of paving the way for others. She divided her time between completing

groundbreaking research and inspiring others to do the same, teaching at both Howard University and Albert Einstein College of Medicine. Marie made it her mission to help students of color enroll in medical schools and graduate from science programs. Her incredible career and her vision for the future changed countless lives.

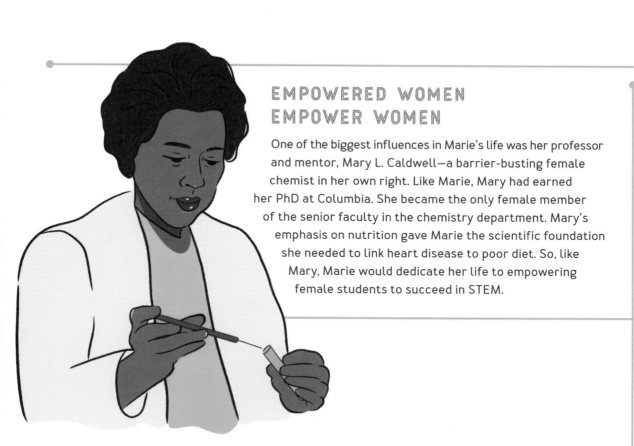

EMPOWERED WOMEN EMPOWER WOMEN

One of the biggest influences in Marie's life was her professor and mentor, Mary L. Caldwell—a barrier-busting female chemist in her own right. Like Marie, Mary had earned her PhD at Columbia. She became the only female member of the senior faculty in the chemistry department. Mary's emphasis on nutrition gave Marie the scientific foundation she needed to link heart disease to poor diet. So, like Mary, Marie would dedicate her life to empowering female students to succeed in STEM.

MARY JACKSON

"For Mary Jackson, life was a long process of raising one's expectations."

—MARGOT LEE SHETTERLY, *HIDDEN FIGURES*

★ PLAYED A VITAL ROLE IN SPACE EXPLORATION AS NASA'S FIRST BLACK FEMALE ENGINEER

★ SPENT HER CAREER AND LIFE EMPOWERING WOMEN TO PURSUE CAREERS IN SCIENCE, ENGINEERING, AND MATHEMATICS

Can you imagine life without laptops and smartphones? Without Google Maps and hourly weather forecasts and FaceTime? If not for a transcontinental competition and some incredible women, you wouldn't have to imagine it. The tech that we take for granted today only exists because of aeronautical engineers like Mary Jackson, who pushed boundaries in both life and science.

With the boundaries imposed on women of color in the 1940s, it's no wonder that Mary had to push. Career options were few and far

SEPARATE AND UNEQUAL

In 1941, President Franklin Delano Roosevelt signed Executive Order 8802, which banned racial discrimination in federal agencies. But that didn't stop Virginia—a state that sits just a few miles from Washington, DC—from continuing to enforce segregation in the workplace. While working to send a man to space, Mary endured the indignity of having to use bathrooms marked "colored" and eating at her desk instead of in the whites-only lunchroom. Despite the vital contributions of Black employees, it wasn't until the mid-1960s that NASA finally integrated their offices.

Mary W. Jackson Nasa HQ

When the Soviet Union launched the first satellite into space in 1957, Americans were stunned. They had been working on a satellite of their own, and yet a war-weakened part of the world had just beaten them to the punch. So American scientists buckled down, launched their satellite, and entered the Space Race. By 1969, Neil Armstrong and Buzz Aldrin were walking on the moon.

Although countries around the world were well on their way to exploring space, the Space Race spurred them to even greater innovation. And that innovation led to all of the tech that we use to communicate, travel, and transport goods today. It also led NASA to recruit talented women of color like Mary Jackson, without whom none of it would have been possible.

between, and Mary explored several of them. She had been a teacher, a tutor, a receptionist, and a bookkeeper. But her intellectual gifts (and dual bachelor's degrees in mathematics and physical science) opened doors for her that she would eventually hold open for others.

In 1951, NASA's predecessor, NACA (the National Advisory Committee for Aeronautics), recruited Mary to a position as a computer. In those days, a *computer* was a research mathematician, not a machine. That meant that Mary and the other women in the West Computers division did complex calculations by hand—and their calculations determined whether a man could make it to space and back in once piece.

This job was important. This job was intense. And this job was small potatoes for Mary Jackson. Fed up

with her "separate and unequal" workplace, she was ready to leave NASA entirely. But a chance encounter with a supervisor changed her mind and her life. Kazimierz Czarnecki patiently listened to Mary's complaints and, recognizing her potential, offered her a spot on his team. He also encouraged her to study to become an engineer.

Some people might think that working at NASA

while raising a family was enough of a challenge. Not Mary. She didn't flinch at the idea of adding graduate-level engineering classes to her evening schedule. Even the fact that the classes were held at an all-white high school didn't stop her. Instead, Mary filed a petition with the court for special permission to attend. Mary's courage in being the first Black student in the program helped her become the first Black female engineer at NASA in 1958.

For two decades, Mary lent her engineering expertise to a variety of departments. She worked with wind tunnels to improve America's planes, published complex scientific papers, and climbed the corporate ladder as far as it would go. But, as a woman of color, she would never be promoted to a management-level position.

MARY'S LEGACY

Mary received plenty of honors and accolades for her leadership and service while she was alive, but she's also earned some incredible honors since her death in 2005. In 2018, a Salt Lake City school that was originally named for slave-owning President Andrew Jackson became Mary W. Jackson Elementary School. And in 2020, NASA renamed its Washington, DC, headquarters The Mary W. Jackson NASA Headquarters. During the announcement, NASA administrator Jim Bridenstine said, "Mary never accepted the status quo; she helped break barriers and open opportunities for African Americans and women in the field of engineering and technology." We're really just beginning to understand and honor that legacy.

Then Mary found the perfect way to keep moving forward—by helping others do it. As a human resources (HR) administrator, she realized she could shape the future of NASA. Mary spent the rest of her days at NASA advising female and minority employees on courses to take and subjects to study to increase their odds of advancement. Technically, the HR position was a demotion. But Mary's sacrifice removed the boundaries for the female scientists, engineers, and mathematicians who came after her.

STEPHANIE KWOLEK

"I tell young people to reach for the stars. And I can't think of a greater high than you could possibly get than by inventing something."

—STEPHANIE KWOLEK

★ INVENTED THE INDUSTRIAL-STRENGTH FIBERS USED IN TIRES, SPACECRAFT, BULLETPROOF VESTS, AND MORE

★ THE ONLY WOMAN SO FAR TO RECEIVE DUPONT'S LAVOISIER MEDAL FOR OUTSTANDING TECHNICAL ACHIEVEMENT

Have you ever noticed that some things have a way of working out for the best? Like, you don't make the soccer team, but that gives you time to do choir, which you end up loving even more. The Dalai Lama XIV put it this way: "Remember that sometimes not getting what you want is a wonderful stroke of luck." Even the biggest disappointments could be making room for something better to come along!

That's certainly how Stephanie Kwolek felt about the curve in her career path. Stephanie was headed to medical school after earning her bachelor's degree in chemistry. But money was tight, and she needed to take a temp job to save up for tuition. A few months into what seemed like a detour, doing research at chemical heavyweight DuPont, Stephanie couldn't imagine doing anything else. She decided to spend her life making discoveries instead of diagnoses.

And it's a good thing, too. If Stephanie had been able to afford that medical degree, she might never have invented Kevlar®, which is one of the only things that stands between soldiers and deadly shrapnel in a combat zone. The fiber is lightweight but also five times as strong as steel, making it the perfect material for bulletproof vests. And that's just one of Kevlar's 200 uses. You can find it in everything from cellphone cables to space suits. But it all started with tires.

In 1965, talk of a fuel shortage led DuPont to challenge employees to find a new high-performance fiber that could make tires lighter and cars more fuel-efficient. Stephanie met that challenge and then some! She discovered that, under certain conditions, polyamide molecules sort of lined up on their own. The result was a *liquid crystalline solution*, which was thin and opalescent—the exact opposite of the clear and syrupy solutions researchers were used to creating.

Stephanie was intrigued by the solution, but not everyone shared her curiosity. You see, to transform a polymer solution from a liquid to

BE A LITTLE BRAVE

Once Stephanie had decided to work in research, she knew she had two options: Gulf or DuPont. She saw more potential at the latter and decided to go for it. When her interviewer told her she'd know his decision in a couple of weeks, she didn't just say, "OK." Instead, she (politely) asked him to move things along because she had another offer to consider. That did the trick—he drew up an offer letter right then and there. Stephanie always believed she got the job at DuPont thanks to that single moment of boldness. Little did she know that it would land her a lifelong career and a legacy of groundbreaking innovation!

a usable fiber, you have to spin it (kind of like cotton candy). And the man who operated the spinneret refused to spin Stephanie's weird-looking solution, thinking it would muck up his machine. It took a few days of persistence, but he finally gave in.

Stephanie knew immediately that the result was something special. The fibers she'd created were stronger and stiffer than any DuPont had ever seen, and it wasn't long before they understood the endless possibilities it offered. Today, you can find Kevlar not only in protective gear and industrial products but also in tennis rackets, canoes, drum sets, and frying pans.

That kind of impact is exactly what Stephanie had in mind when she dedicated her life to discovery. "When I look back on my career, I'm inspired most by the fact that I was fortunate enough to do something that would be of benefit to mankind," she said. "I don't think there's anything like saving someone's life to bring you satisfaction and happiness."

Stephanie officially retired from DuPont in 1986, but that didn't stop her from putting in her two cents as needed. She spent the rest of her time tutoring students in chemistry and trying to get kids excited about careers in science. (You might even get to perform her "Nylon Rope Trick" in class!) Stephanie's inventions have saved countless lives, and her contagious love of discovery has changed countless more.

RIGHT BRAIN OR LEFT?

Being a scientist doesn't mean being analytical all the time. Plenty of creative minds find homes in scientific fields. Stephanie is a perfect example. When she was little, she wanted to follow her seamstress mom into fashion. She may never have designed dresses, but her work as a chemist has had a huge impact on the clothing and uniform industries. Stephanie's inventions help protect firefighters from head to toe—their boots and helmets are made with Kevlar, and their suits are made with flame-resistant Nomex®. Stephanie also had a hand in creating Lycra®, the stretchy material used in everything from swimsuits to yoga pants. By choosing a career in chemistry, she got to enjoy a sense of discovery and wonder at work every day.

VERA RUBIN, PHD

"Don't let anyone keep you down for silly reasons such as who you are."

—VERA RUBIN

★ HELPED PROVE THE EXISTENCE OF DARK MATTER, THE GLUE THAT HOLDS THE UNIVERSE TOGETHER

★ THE FIRST FEMALE ASTRONOMER TO HAVE A US OBSERVATORY NAMED AFTER HER

After thousands of years of scientific study and advancements, there's still so much we don't know about the universe we live in. Even the best telescopes in the world can only see so far, the best labs can only analyze so much. And for astronomers like Vera Rubin, that's exactly what's so exciting about the field—the awe-inspiring possibilities.

For as long as she could remember, Vera had been fascinated by the stars. She'd stay up past her bedtime just to stare out her window, mesmerized by their movements. "Even then I was more interested in the question than in the answer," she said. Vera would end up finding some incredible

answers anyway. And she'd do it in spite of too many men telling her she shouldn't even be asking the questions.

Although astronomy was a tough field for women to break into in the 1940s, Vera knew it could be done because of fellow Science Superstar Maria Mitchell (see page 13). She even followed in Maria's footsteps by going to Vassar College for her bachelor's degree in the subject. But Vera still had to deal with sexist attitudes throughout her education and career.

When Vera requested a catalog from Princeton's all-male graduate school, she heard crickets. When she arrived at

Although Vera traversed galaxies at work, she said her biggest challenge was childcare. She and her husband raised four children while both pursuing demanding educations and careers in science. Vera was devoted to her children, but she hated to step away from astronomy for too long. So, in the early years of her career, she worked parttime—and often from her dining room table—to be home with her kids. That turned out to be a winning strategy for everyone; all four of her children hold PhDs in the natural sciences, crediting their mom with making a life of science seem like fun.

Cornell for her master's degree in astronomy, a male professor told her to study something else. In Georgetown's PhD program, her male adviser not-so-graciously offered to present her thesis work as his own.

Vera never let sexism stop her, though. She ignored anyone who tried to chase her away from astronomy, presented her thesis herself, and earned her PhD in astronomy. And in 1965, Vera became the first woman admitted to California's prestigious Palomar Observatory. Even then, the men in charge weren't crazy about giving her access. That didn't worry Vera one bit. In fact, she encouraged them to get used to the idea by sticking a paper skirt over the male stick figure on the observatory's bathroom door.

With access to better equipment, Vera was able to observe that

galaxies didn't move the way scientists assumed they would. Stars should have been flying off in all directions without gravity to hold them together at the ends. Instead, they continued to rotate at the same speed no matter where they were in the lineup. Some other invisible force, she realized, must be hard at work.

That force was dark matter, which we now know comprises around 84% of the universe's material. Think of it like the air we breathe: although we can't see it, we can feel it all around us, and we know that it keeps us alive. Dark matter affects everything in the universe and how it all moves.

The existence of such invisible matter was just a theory before Vera came along. Through years of observation and data

Palomar Observatory

collection, she was able to prove it. Her work revolutionized the field of physics and our understanding of how the universe works.

Vera's history-making contribution to science should have made her a shoo-in for the Nobel Prize, but she never made it past the shortlist. Many in the field feel that this was an unforgivable oversight rooted in sexism. Out of more than 200 Nobel Laureates in Physics, only four have been women.

Vera never spoke about the Nobel snub, but the lack of women in science infuriated her. It's something she worked her whole life to correct. Whenever she saw a lack of female speakers at a conference, she would call up the organizers and tell them they had a problem they needed to fix. She also urged the National Academy of Sciences to admit more female members and personally mentored female scientists. Vera understood what many scientists today still don't: science's possibilities are only endless when they're possible for *everyone*.

ANYBODY OUT THERE?

Vera was a firm believer in the idea that human beings aren't alone in the universe. When asked about the possibility in a 2001 interview, she answered, "We know that the laws of physics are virtually the same all over the universe." With 200 billion stars in our galaxy and billions of galaxies, she reasoned, it would be impossible for there not to be other planets and solar systems like ours. But don't count on alien invasions any time soon—the next life-sustaining solar system is probably light-years away.

TU YOUYOU

"Every scientist dreams of doing something that can help the world."

—TU YOUYOU

★ SAVED MILLIONS OF LIVES THROUGH HER DISCOVERY AND ISOLATION OF ARTEMISININ, THE FIRST LINE OF DEFENSE AGAINST DEADLY MALARIA

★ THE FIRST CHINESE WOMAN TO WIN A NOBEL PRIZE

Some people are born inspired. Others need a little push in the right direction. Unfortunately for Tu Youyou, that push was a painful bout of tuberculosis (a serious infectious disease that usually affects the lungs). But by the time Youyou returned to high school healthy, she knew what she wanted to do with her life: find cures for diseases like the one she'd just endured.

Youyou's first move was to study pharmacology at Beijing Medical College, where she learned how to classify medicinal plants, extract active ingredients, and determine chemical structures. She then spent several years working at the Academy of Traditional Chinese Medicine and taking a course for researchers trained in modern Western methods. Years later, the Chinese government would come knocking, in need of Youyou's unique skill set.

In 1969, China was in the middle of a political revolution led by communist leader Mao Zedong. But Mao had decided that malaria (a deadly disease spread by mosquitoes) was as big and immediate a national threat as capitalism. He recruited Youyou to lead mission 523, the super-secret government project he'd formed to find a cure.

Youyou traveled to the tropical Chinese island of Hainan, where a malaria outbreak was devastating the local population. Because of the revolution, Youyou's husband had already been sent to work in the countryside. That meant she had to leave her 1-year-old daughter with her parents and put her 4-year-old daughter in a nursery. She wouldn't see her daughters again for 3 years, but Youyou felt she had a duty to her country and her people.

NO, NO, NO

In China, Youyou has been called the "Three Nos" Nobel Prize winner: she has no medical degree, no doctorate, and no experience working overseas. Only a dozen women have ever won the Nobel Prize in medicine. For Youyou to win it without a doctorate or medical degree to her name makes her one of the most extraordinary figures among them. But you'd never know it to talk to her. Despite her incredible contribution to medicine, Youyou has tried to stay out of the spotlight. She believes that knowing she helped save lives is reward enough.

By this time, researchers around the world had tried more than 240,000 compounds to treat malaria. But many had been relying on Western medicine. Youyou and her team, on the other hand, turned to ancient Chinese medical texts from the Zhou, Qing, and Han dynasties for answers.

They finally homed in on a reference to sweet wormwood, which had been used around 400 CE to treat "intermittent fevers"—a symptom of malaria. Catching that subtle clue paid off. Artemisinin, the active compound in wormwood, worked wonders on malaria-friendly parasites. Its extracts, however, weren't doing the trick on malaria itself.

Youyou went back to the drawing board. After rereading the ancient text, she had a thought: maybe the heat used to extract the artemisinin was damaging it. By using ether-based solvent, which boils at a lower temperature, she was able to preserve the compound.

Suddenly, Youyou was seeing a 100% success rate in animal trials. But to find out how the compound worked on humans, she'd have to take it herself. She saw this sacrifice as her

Eastern practices, and vice versa. But the more we learn, the more we understand the benefits of integrating both. Youyou believes that's where the biggest potential for advances in medicine lies.

The next time you notice that you're not getting anywhere, take a minute and a deep breath. Then zoom out. What might you be missing? What lessons can you learn from others? Keep an open mind, and you'll always be able to find the answers.

responsibility as head of the research group. Luckily, the treatment worked just as well on her as it had on monkeys and mice. And it worked miracles in the 21 malaria patients who received the treatment next—everyone recovered.

Today, the World Health Organization (WHO) recommends artemisinin combination therapy as the first line of defense against malaria. The Lasker Foundation called Youyou's contribution "arguably the most important pharmaceutical intervention in the last half-century." But Youyou saw it as "a gift from traditional Chinese medicine to the world." In 2015, she became the first Chinese woman to receive the Nobel Prize in Physiology and Medicine.

Youyou's success is a lesson for all scientists: answers to your biggest questions can come from anywhere. In the past, people who studied Western medicine have been skeptical of

WHAT'S IN A NAME?

Youyou's dad named her after a line of poetry found in the *Chinese Book of Odes*. Loosely translated, it reads, "deer bleat 'youyou' while they are eating the wild Hao." Although naming someone after the sounds a deer makes while eating may seem a bit unusual, the verse turned out to be prophetic. *Hao* refers to *artemisia*. Sound familiar? It's the genus of plants that includes wormwood, from which Youyou extracted the cure: artemisinin. The answer to Youyou's greatest question was with her from the start.

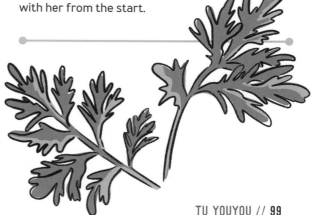

JANE GOODALL

"What you do makes a difference. And you have to decide what kind of difference you want to make."

—JANE GOODALL

★ TRANSFORMED OUR UNDERSTANDING OF CHIMPANZEES AND THEIR RELATIONSHIP TO HUMANS

★ HAS EMPOWERED A NEW GENERATION OF CONSERVATIONISTS THROUGH EDUCATION AND VOLUNTEER PROGRAMS ALL OVER THE WORLD

In 1960, Jane Goodall made one of the most significant scientific discoveries of the 20th century. She didn't do it by spending hours in a sterilized lab, gloved and frowning and peering through microscopes. She did it by climbing barefoot through trees, handing out bananas, and letting her emotions run the show. In other words, she did it her way.

Jane is one of the lucky few who discover their life's purpose early on. After reading Edgar Rice Burroughs' book *Tarzan of the Apes* (and being thoroughly disappointed to share a name with Tarzan's "wimpy" love interest), ten-year-old Jane knew what she wanted. When she grew up, she said, she would "go to Africa, live with animals, and write books about them." But pursuing that dream wasn't easy.

This was 1944, when the world was at war, money was tight, and girls didn't go adventuring in mysterious jungles. Many well-meaning people told Jane to dream smaller. But not Jane's mom. She said, "Jane, if you really want something and you work hard and you take advantage of opportunity and you never give up, you will find a way." And Jane did find a way.

With just secretarial school under her belt, Jane jumped at an opportunity to work for respected paleoanthropologist Dr. Louis Leakey. He saw her passion and drive and offered her an even better break: to live with and write about chimpanzees in Africa. She arrived in Gombe at the age of 26 and got right to work.

Today, anyone who's watched cat videos knows that animals have their own personalities, emotions, and ways of communicating. Jane knew it then. But in the 1960s, the compassionate approach she took to studying chimpanzees was unique. While other researchers treated animals like unthinking spores in a lab, Jane observed them with empathy and respect.

and extracted the bugs for a tasty snack. (Yum!) Chimpanzees, it turned out, made and used tools.

This finding was a jaw-dropping breakthrough in the scientific community. In the days before Jane's discovery, scientists believed that the use of tools made human beings superior to all other creatures. But the more Jane observed chimpanzees, the more she discovered what we have in common with them.

Chimpanzees love, have families, adopt orphans, observe rituals, and even wage wars. They kiss, hug, hold hands, pat each other on the back, get into spats, and shake their fists in anger. By tapping into her own emotions, Jane understood theirs. And these revelations, she says, "eventually persuaded science to come out of its little, tight box, and realize we are part of, not separate from, the rest of the animal kingdom."

It took 2 years and a lot of bananas, but Jane's patience paid off. She got close enough to watch as the apes stripped twigs of their leaves, slipped them into termite mounds,

OUR FUZZY COUSINS

Chimpanzees, gorillas, orangutans, and bonobos are all part of the same family, called great apes. And guess what—so are we! In fact, we share 98.6% of our DNA with chimps. That's why learning about their habits, relationships, environment, and response to disease is so important. Understanding chimpanzees helps us better understand human beings.

It's this connection that informed Jane's next move. By the 1980s, deforestation and animal trafficking had landed chimpanzees on the endangered species list. So, what began with a dream ended with a mission. Jane had to save the chimpanzees. "I couldn't just stay in Gombe, watching chimpanzees leading an idyllic life," she says. "I had to try and do whatever I could." And that meant traveling the world, advocating for wildlife conservation.

Decades later, Jane continues to spend 300 days per year on the road, educating people about wildlife. Her nonprofit organization, the Jane Goodall Institute for Wildlife Research, Education and Conservation, has organized conservation programs all over the world. And Gombe has become Gombe National Park, an area of protected land in Tanzania.

One of Jane's main priorities is empowering a new generation of conservationists, saying, "There is a powerful force unleashed when young people resolve to make a change." Ready to unleash your power? Check out www.rootsandshoots.org to find a chapter near you and help Jane save the world!

"Every individual matters. Every individual has a role to play. Every individual makes a difference."

—JANE GOODALL

EYES ON THE REAL PRIZE

Over the last five decades, Jane has earned an incredible number of honors and awards. She's also been named a Messenger of Peace by the United Nations and a Dame of the British Empire by Queen Elizabeth II herself. Although the fancy titles are nice, Jane's more interested in the prize money that accompanied some of those awards. She knows how much good each dollar can do in the world, which is why she uses that money to fund her work. So far, it's helped protect 5,000 chimpanzees and gorillas, support 130 communities worldwide, and empower 4,900 groups of kids to change the world.

SYLVIA EARLE, PHD

"The best scientists and explorers have the attributes of kids. They ask questions and have a sense of wonder. They have curiosity. Who, what, where, why, when, and how!"

—SYLVIA EARLE

★ *TIME* MAGAZINE'S FIRST "HERO FOR THE PLANET" AND THE FIRST FEMALE CHIEF SCIENTIST OF THE US NATIONAL OCEANIC AND ATMOSPHERIC ADMINISTRATION (NOAA)

★ PIONEERED THE STUDY OF MARINE ECOSYSTEMS AND THE ENVIRONMENTAL IMPACT OF POLLUTION

A CLOSE CALL

In 1977, Sylvia had what she called a "heart-stopping moment." She and two underwater cinematographers had convinced four scientific organizations to let them get into the water with whales. Sylvia watched in awe as five humpback whales gracefully glided and swirled through the water around her. But then one headed straight for her diving partner, who was too busy filming to notice. Sylvia yelled warnings as the whale passed by the cinematographer, lifting its flipper over his head at the last moment. The whales, Sylvia realized, knew exactly what they were doing. With that, she finally relaxed and enjoyed one of the most magical dives of her life.

Imagine growing up with brothers and doing everything they do. You play baseball in the backyard, do cannonballs off the high dive, ride bikes around the neighborhood. Now imagine that, when you're older, someone tells you that your brothers can have their pick of jobs, but you have to choose from just a handful. Because you're a girl. That would be pretty crazy, right?

That's what women like Sylvia Earle faced in the 1950s. She and her brothers had loving and supportive parents who helped them

A PIONEERING TEST CASE

Tektite was actually a trial run for Skylab, the first US space station. Scientists wanted to see how researchers did when confined together in a "hostile environment" over an extended period of time (but without the expense and bother of actually going into space). By participating in the project, Sylvia helped lay the foundation for missions that would further our understanding of space.

believe they could do anything. But when Sylvia got older, she noticed her mom's definition of "anything" narrow. Suddenly, it meant being a teacher, a nurse, or a stewardess, instead of being a superintendent, a doctor, or a pilot. "It was just the way things were," she says.

But, after spending her childhood exploring the outdoors, Sylvia had her heart set on a career in oceanography. It didn't matter to her that she was often the only woman in class, or that people seemed baffled by her talent for science. She couldn't imagine doing anything else.

Since then, Sylvia has spent more than 7,000 hours underwater, set diving records, and led more than 100 expeditions in every part of the world. In 1970, she led the first all-female team to live underwater in the Tektite II experiment. Although they were met with sexist headlines and skepticism, the female aquanauts proved they were every bit the serious scientists their male colleagues were.

Sylvia and her team spent two weeks in the water off the US Virgin Islands getting up close and personal with the ocean's inhabitants. "The fish were curious about us," she said. And their curiosity allowed the women to get close. Sylvia was able to see that the fish had not just characteristics, but also personalities of their own. She watched them go about their lives like you might watch people from a park bench.

The Tektite project made Sylvia want to spend even more time underwater, and to protect the things she discovered there. Although the ocean covers more than 70% of our world, 95% of it is completely unknown to us. The parts we can see, though, have changed drastically in the last 50 years alone. When Sylvia started diving, the waters were clean and fish were abundant. Today, we have garbage patches and dead zones that can't support life, not to mention drastically reduced fish populations thanks to pollution and overfishing.

Sylvia has spent her career making sure we understand why ocean conservation is important. It's not just because of the creatures that could be lost, like the lobsters and horseshoe crabs that have been roaming the oceans since before the dinosaurs. It's also because healthy oceans are essential to human existence.

The ocean is home to most of the life on Earth. It serves as a source of food and travel, but it also controls the weather and the climate. And it happens to provide 20% of the oxygen we breathe. That's why Sylvia poured her experience into Mission Blue, a nonprofit devoted to exploring and protecting essential marine habitats. Her work helps ensure that we can all enjoy the beauty and wonder that exists beneath the water's surface for years to come.

GET INVOLVED TODAY!

Sylvia believes we need to "take care of the systems that take care of us," and that getting people to care about them is the first step. She's given talks and interviews all over the world, written nearly 200 papers and several books, and shared her experiences on social media to make sure that we all know what's at stake. Want to learn more about her mission and how you can help? Follow @SylviaEarle on Twitter!

SAU LAN WU, PHD

"You believe in yourself.
You hold true to your determination.
And you will do something great."

—SAU LAN WU

★ HELPED CONFIRM THE EXISTENCE OF THREE FUNDAMENTAL PARTICLES (AND COUNTING), INCLUDING THE HIGGS BOSON

★ HAS MADE IT HER MISSION TO MENTOR AND PLACE PHD STUDENTS FOR SUCCESS IN THE FIELD

If there's anything we can learn from our Superstars, it's that their contribution to science is usually just one of the ways in which they've changed the world. Sau Lan Wu's research has helped us learn more about the tiny parts of matter that make up the world around us. But her life is a lesson in the power of compassion and support.

Sau Lan was born in the slums of Hong Kong at the height of World War II and the Japanese invasion of China. While her mom and brother slept in a small rented bedroom, she slept in the hallway of a local rice shop. And every day, her mom made it clear to her that education was the way out.

Having grown up poor and a woman in Hong Kong, Sau Lan's mom wasn't allowed to attend school. She relied entirely on Sau Lan's father for what little money she had. Seeing how helpless that made her mom feel, Sau Lan decided she was going to stand on her own

CERN GLOBE

two feet. She picked 50 random names out of a book of US colleges and universities and applied to them all.

Only one school responded with the full scholarship Sau Lan needed, and it happened to be one of the top women's schools in the nation. Vassar College gave her everything she'd need to succeed. Alumnae helped her travel to the school, Vassar covered her books and school supplies, and fellow students donated clothing. Thanks to all of that support, Sau Lan was able to graduate with honors in just 3 years.

After earning her master's and PhD from Harvard, Sau Lan became a research associate at MIT, where she made her first great discovery: the charm quark. A quark is an elementary particle—it makes up larger particles, like protons and neutrons, which make up atoms. And atoms make up,

well, everything else, from the stars in the sky to the socks on your feet. Finding one of these tiny particles was a very big deal.

Sau Lan did it again a few years later when she discovered gluon, an elementary particle that holds quarks together like glue (hence the name). But she topped both of those finds with one more: the Higgs boson particle. Scientists had been trying to uncover this particle—the

TUNE EM OUT

When Sau Lan made the monthlong boat trip to the United States, she was all alone and barely spoke English. She bravely pushed herself to talk to the other passengers so that she could do well at school. She also arrived in America in 1960, at the height of segregation. Faced with bathrooms marked "white" and "colored" during a trip to Virginia, Sau Lan realized she didn't know where she stood. Her race, like her gender, would always be a sticking point for some people. As Sau Lan said, "In the end, you have to be immune to this kind of criticism. What they don't see is that I'm successful because I try very hard. I work for it, totally devote myself, my life, to my job."

most elementary of elementary particles—for decades. Without it, the universe would be nothing and we humans wouldn't exist.

And Sau Lan found it using one of the coolest pieces of equipment known to particle physicists. The Large Hadron Collider is a 17-mile-long particle accelerator that was built 300 feet underground at the legendary CERN research lab in Geneva, Switzerland, which is where Sau Lan works today. Having a machine like this at her fingertips means that Sau Lan's search for elemental particles is far from over.

But even more important to Sau Lan than finding the next elementary particle is ensuring that her students at CERN have the chance to make even bigger discoveries. She has not only mentored dozens of students through their PhDs, but she has also helped place them at prestigious labs and universities all over the United States. Sau Lan has a knack for knowing what will help each student succeed, and she does everything in her power to put them on the right path.

Sau Lan still prizes her independence, but she's also learned the value of a support system. Having people who cared made all the difference for her at Vassar, and now she pays that forward to her students at CERN. Who knows how many more Science Superstars exist thanks to her encouragement!

BETTER TOGETHER

Despite (or maybe because of) many quiet nights spent alone at libraries and labs throughout her education, Sau Lan is a big believer in collaboration at work. The more people on a project, the better, she says. A larger team means having more people to learn from, to bounce ideas off, and to challenge you to do better. It also means that each person can focus on doing what they do best—no multitasking necessary. Sau Lan credits the support and expertise of her teams for all three of her big discoveries.

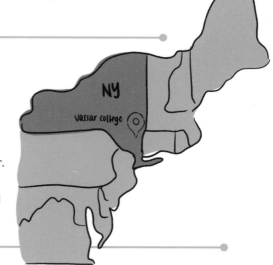

ALEXA CANADY, MD

"If you want to be something, you have to perceive that something is possible."

—ALEXA CANADY

★ THE FIRST BLACK FEMALE NEUROSURGEON IN THE UNITED STATES, AND THE FIRST TO BE CERTIFIED BY THE AMERICAN BOARD OF NEUROLOGICAL SURGERY

★ HER RESEARCH LED TO THE INVENTION OF THE PROGRAMMABLE ANTISIPHON SHUNT TO TREAT HYDROCEPHALUS

You won't find a single person who hasn't had to overcome an obstacle (or several) on the way to achieving something great. But sometimes, the biggest obstacle you face is you. How you talk to yourself has a huge impact on your life. Tell yourself you can't do something, and odds are pretty good that you won't even try.

That's a lesson that Alexa Canady had to learn. She overcame racism, sexism, and the challenges of medical school and residency to become the first Black female neurosurgeon in the United States. But Alexa herself has said, "The greatest challenge I faced in becoming a neurosurgeon was believing it was possible." Getting out of her own way was the first step to having the life and career she dreamed of.

Alexa got those big dreams from her parents, who both believed anything was possible with the right education. They taught her never to let anything stop her from reaching her potential. When she and her brother were the only two Black students in school, her mom told her, "So what if you're the token Black girl? Take that token and spend it." With her parents' encouragement, Alexa graduated from high school with honors.

But Alexa almost stopped herself again in college. While studying math at the University of Michigan, she had a "crisis of confidence" and nearly dropped out. Then she heard about a minority scholarship for medicine and felt like fate had intervened. She had found something worth stepping out of her own way for.

them wrong, accepting an internship at Yale-New Haven Hospital before moving on to residency at the University of Minnesota.

After seeing the joy and resilience of the kids in the pediatric ward, Alexa chose to specialize in pediatric neurosurgery. "It never ceased to amaze me how happy the children were," she says. Kids are also naturally more open and accepting. But Alexa wasn't so sure how the parents of her patients would react to having a neurosurgeon who was both Black and a woman. Turns out, she didn't need to worry. Alexa's warm personality made her a favorite in the neurosurgery department.

In medical school, Alexa felt like her professors were ignoring the female students. That just made her work harder to stand out. Then her advisers warned her away from neurosurgery—the specialty she had fallen in love with—because it would be too hard for a Black woman to find work. She built up an unbeatable résumé and proved

PATIENTS FIRST

You have to be pretty confident to be successful in the incredibly competitive field of neurosurgery, which might be why neurosurgeons (and surgeons in general) have a bit of a reputation for big egos. But Alexa made sure that she and her colleagues kept their egos in check and put patient care first. "In order to provide good-quality care," she says, "it is so important that patients are able to talk to you and not regard you as some deity above them." With everything she'd accomplished, Alexa had every right to feel like an authority. But she preferred to play video games with her patients and put them at ease instead. And that's what made hers one of the best departments of pediatric neurosurgery in the country.

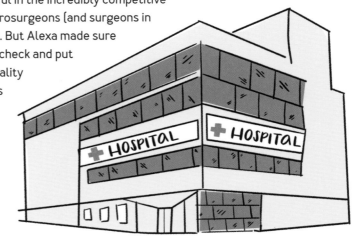

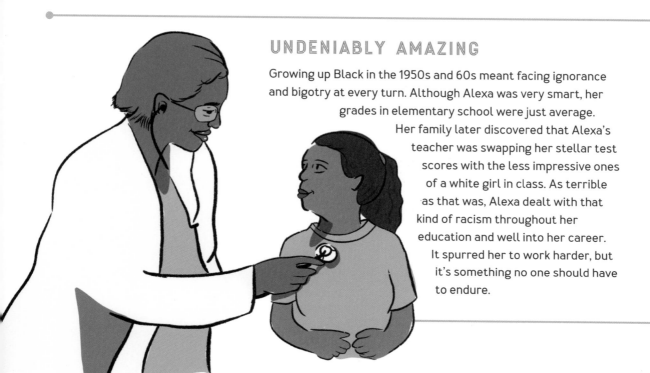

UNDENIABLY AMAZING

Growing up Black in the 1950s and 60s meant facing ignorance and bigotry at every turn. Although Alexa was very smart, her grades in elementary school were just average. Her family later discovered that Alexa's teacher was swapping her stellar test scores with the less impressive ones of a white girl in class. As terrible as that was, Alexa dealt with that kind of racism throughout her education and well into her career. It spurred her to work harder, but it's something no one should have to endure.

Although some surgeons prefer to keep patients at arm's length, Alexa built relationships with them all, earning a reputation for compassion and kindness. That unique approach to patient care earned Alexa as job as director of neurosurgery at Michigan's Children's Hospital when she was just 36 years old. With Alexa at the helm, the department became known as one of the best in the country.

Between performing surgeries and running an entire department, Alexa had a pretty full plate. Still, she found the time to teach and do research at Wayne State University.

Her work there led to the invention of the programmable antisiphon shunt, a device used to treat hydrocephalus (a painful build-up of fluid in the brain).

Alexa moved to Florida with her husband in 2001 for a well-deserved retirement, but she didn't sit still for long. She worked part time at Pensacola's Sacred Heart Hospital until her second attempt at retirement in 2012. Today, Alexa advocates for women in medicine, speaking at local schools and events to inspire the next generation of neurosurgeons to move past their self-doubt and reach their own potential.

SALLY RIDE, PHD

"Young girls need to see role models in whatever careers they may choose, just so they can picture themselves doing those jobs someday. You can't be what you can't see."

—SALLY RIDE

★ THE YOUNGEST PERSON AND THE FIRST AMERICAN WOMAN TO TRAVEL TO SPACE

★ FOUNDED SALLY RIDE SCIENCE TO ENCOURAGE WOMEN AND GIRLS TO PURSUE CAREERS IN STEM

Have you ever been scared to tell someone you changed your mind? Changing course when you're on the wrong path doesn't make you indecisive. It shows that you're smart enough to adjust to new information (even if that new information is "I thought I'd like cheesesteak pizza, but I really don't"). And although it takes courage to make a change, it's often worth it. You never know what amazing things are waiting for you on your new path.

Famed astronaut Sally Ride thought she was going to be a professional tennis player. She was nationally ranked and even left Swarthmore College her sophomore year to pursue her dream. But 3 months in, she decided that school was a better fit for her. Changing her mind turned out to be the best thing she could have done.

By attending Stanford University for her bachelor's, master's, and PhD in physics, Sally changed the course of her life and the course of the US space program. At Stanford, she saw a newspaper ad for NASA, which was looking for new recruits. And NASA was allowing women to apply for the first time since the start of the space program.

Sally beat out thousands of applicants to become one of 35 astronauts—only six of whom were women—in the class of 1978. And

NO BIG DEAL

To become the first American woman in space, Sally first had to meet NASA's extensive list of requirements and pass its grueling training program (which included parachute jumps and water-survival training). She trained for 5 years before being assigned to her first mission. But when she went into space, all the media wanted to know was what kind of makeup she'd be taking. She said at the time, "It's too bad this is such a big deal. It's too bad our society isn't further along." Today, more than 40 women have followed in Sally's space-traveling footsteps, and it's because she helped normalize the idea of women in science.

in June of 1983, she made history by becoming the youngest person and the first American woman to go into space. She worked as a mission specialist and the resident expert in robotic arms aboard the *Challenger* space shuttle, helping to put satellites out into space.

Sally loved her time in space, saying, "The thing that I'll remember most about the flight is that it was fun. In fact, I'm sure it was the most fun I'll ever have in my life." She was thrilled to go up again the following year for an 8-day voyage. This time, she conducted scientific observations of Earth and worked on refueling techniques for space shuttles.

Little did Sally know it would be her last mission in space. Just after the *Challenger* launched for its tenth mission, it broke apart in midair, killing all seven crew members. She joined the presidential commission that investigated the accident before turning her focus to administrative work at NASA and becoming the first director of NASA's Office of Exploration.

After retiring from NASA in 1987, Sally joined the faculty at the University

> *"All adventures, especially into new territory, are scary."*
>
> —SALLY RIDE

of California, San Diego, as a physics professor and director of the California Space Institute. But she soon embarked on a new, more personal mission: to inspire the next generation of scientists. She helped NASA create educational outreach programs for kids, like EarthKAM, which allows middle-school students to take pictures of Earth using a camera on the International Space Station.

Sally wanted to make science education more fun and engaging, and she wanted to show little girls everywhere that they could do amazing things with their love of science. In addition to her work with NASA, she coauthored several children's books and gave talks at schools to share the incredible experiences she had in space. And in 2001, she founded Sally Ride Science, an organization dedicated to inspiring kids—and especially young girls—to participate in STEM.

After Sally lost her long battle with pancreatic cancer, she received the Medal of Freedom from President Barack Obama. Her partner of 27 years in life and business, Tam O'Shaughnessy, accepted the award on her behalf and has continued to work toward Sally's goal of encouraging women and girls in STEM. Even though she's gone, Sally is still inspiring people to reach for the stars.

THE COST OF SEXISM

Sally was the first *American* woman in space, but she wasn't the first woman. That honor belongs to Soviet cosmonaut Valentina Tereshkova, who floated weightlessly among the stars in 1963. Around the same time, a group of 13 women participated in an American program designed to test whether women were fit for space travel. They passed with flying colors, but NASA still wasn't wild about the idea of women in the program. That institutional sexism kept America lagging behind the Soviet Union unnecessarily for a full 20 years.

MAE JEMISON, MD

"Never limit yourself because of others' limited imagination; never limit others because of your own limited imagination."

—MAE JEMISON

★ THE FIRST BLACK WOMAN ADMITTED TO THE ASTRONAUT TRAINING PROGRAM AND THE FIRST TO TRAVEL TO SPACE

★ FOUNDED THE JEMISON GROUP, WHICH ADVOCATES FOR SCIENCE LITERACY AND SUSTAINABILITY

Reading about some of these remarkable women can be pretty intimidating at times. Mae Jemison, for example, is a doctor, a Peace Corps volunteer, a dancer, a teacher, an astronaut, and the founder and CEO of multiple organizations. Oh, and she speaks four languages.

How do you live up to an example like that? Easy. You live up to Mae's example by following your heart the way she followed hers, the way all of the Superstars have. That's it. And when you read about her accomplishments, notice that she took things just one step at a time.

Mae was just 5 years old when she declared to her class that she wanted to be a scientist. It was an odd choice for a little Black girl in 1961—a time when people of color were still treated as second-class citizens—but Mae was resolved. Then watching *Star Trek* inspired an even bigger dream: to go to space. Although Mae would find her way to NASA, she didn't walk a straight path.

By the time she finished high school, Mae had discovered a love of dance, acted in plays, and joined the cheerleading squad. She also spent long hours in the library, reading everything she could about women in science. (Madeleine L'Engle's *A Wrinkle in Time*, with its female heroines, was one of her favorites.)

Mae started at Stanford University when she was just 16 years old. Some girls would have been scared to leave home so early, but Mae was focused on soaking up more of her many interests, like choreography and student government. She even graduated with two very different degrees, one in chemical engineering and the other in African and African American studies. And then she headed for medical school at Cornell University.

Being a medical student at an Ivy League school couldn't have been easy, and Mae still

FEARLESS

Take a look at all of Mae's accomplishments, and you can tell that she's fearless. (You have to be pretty fearless to let yourself be launched into space!) And she says she can trace that bravery back to a single day. She was 12 years old, and she was watching National Guardsmen march through her mostly Black Chicago neighborhood with rifles. They had been called in by the mayor to prevent civil rights demonstrations (aka to intimidate people of color) before an important political meeting. Mae remembers feeling scared and angry, but she also remembers feeling determined. She realized that she belonged in America every bit as much as those Guardsmen. Mae made herself a promise that day never to let anything or *anyone* make her feel that afraid again.

DO IT ALL

We're often told to focus on one thing, but you never know when having multiple interests will come in handy. Although Mae's almost-career as a dancer may seem totally unrelated to her actual career in science, the physical fitness it required was a major factor in being considered for astronaut training. Your body has to be able to withstand immense physical stress from, among other things, being launched at top speed into outer space. Through dance class, Mae says, she "grew stronger and gained an appreciation for hard work, physical strength, and grace." The lesson here: pursue everything that piques your curiosity! It could be the key to following your dreams.

found time to study in Cuba and Kenya and to volunteer at a Cambodian refugee camp in Thailand. That wanderlust would also influence her career. After just a couple of years in general medicine, Mae joined the Peace Corps as a medical officer to work in Liberia and Sierra Leone. But, inspired by fellow Superstar Sally Ride, Mae eventually circled back to her childhood dream of being an astronaut.

Mae joined NASA's astronaut training program in 1987. Five years later, she became the first Black woman to travel to space, orbiting the Earth for 8 days on the space shuttle *Endeavour*. Mae conducted a variety of experiments in space on things like bone cells, tadpole growth, and weightlessness and motion sickness among the crew. And she started every shift by saying, "Hailing frequencies

open," a quote from the TV show that sparked her interest in space.

Mae came back to the Kennedy Space Center with a renewed sense of purpose, but that purpose didn't involve space travel anymore. She resigned from NASA in 1993. Since then, she's taught at both Dartmouth and Cornell, founded her own sustainable-technology consulting firm and nonprofit organization, created outreach programs for students in STEM, and headed an initiative to make travel beyond our solar system possible. (She also got to guest star on *Star Trek*!)

If you think about it, Mae isn't amazing because she went to medical school or volunteered in Africa or conducted experiments in space. (Well, not *just* because of those things.) She's amazing because she set goals, worked hard, overcame obstacles, and lived the life she wanted to live. And you can do that, too.

JENNIFER DOUDNA, PHD

"The more we know, the more we realize there is to know."

—JENNIFER DOUDNA

★ COFOUNDER OF FIVE BIOTECH FIRMS THAT USE CRISPR, THE TOOL SHE HELPED DISCOVER THAT CAN EDIT DNA SEQUENCES

★ A MENTOR, A LEADER, A SERIAL ENTREPRENEUR, A NOBEL LAUREATE, AND ONE OF THE WORLD'S MOST SOUGHT—AFTER SCIENTISTS

Especially in America, we can have pretty narrow ideas of what certain careers look like. A lawyer works with clients and presents cases in court. A doctor treats patients in a clinic or hospital. A scientist works in a lab or teaches in a school. But the truth is, there are as many ways to build a career as there are stars in the sky. And if you're lucky and you're honest with yourself about what actually makes you happy, you can design the career you want.

Jennifer realized that when she was in her early forties and well into her career as professor of biochemistry and molecular biology at the University of California, Berkeley. After running her lab at Berkeley for

15 years, she suddenly couldn't imagine doing it for the next 15. She wanted to do more than research—she wanted to solve problems.

Jennifer thought maybe she'd go to medical school. Then she saw a neighbor start his own company and

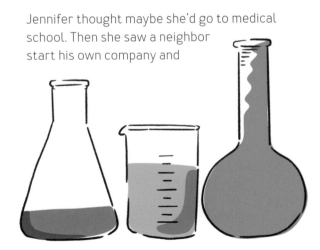

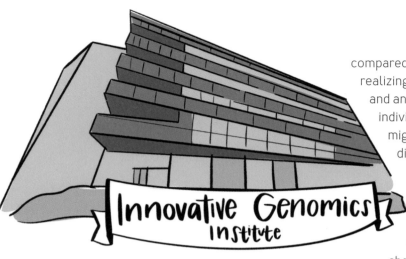

Innovative Genomics
Institute

compared notes and had a breakthrough, realizing that they could use CRISPR and an enzyme called Cas9 to cut out individual genes. And that meant they might be able to cut out genetic diseases, too.

This was a huge revelation. "Human beings have now learned enough about our own genetic code that we can change it at will," she says about the discovery. "It's kind of crazy to think about." Suddenly everyone in the world was thinking about it. And in 2020, the pair won a Nobel Prize for it.

considered business school, but she landed in a job leading discovery research at Genentech. Yet, 2 months in, she realized she missed the freedom of academia. That's when Jennifer had the brilliant idea to design the work she wanted. She went back to Berkeley, but she nixed all of the things that annoyed her (travel, classes, committees) and focused on the fun stuff: discovery.

That reshuffling of her career gave Jennifer the time and drive to look into CRISPR (short for *clustered regularly interspaced short palindromic repeats*). CRISPR are basically little bits of repeating genetic code in bacteria that sandwich bits of DNA left over from viruses that once infected the bacteria. Scientists at the time knew CRISPR existed, but they didn't fully understand how they worked.

Jennifer was trying to figure that out when she ran into French microbiologist Emmanuelle Charpentier at a conference. The pair

A DOUBLE-EDGED SWORD

Jennifer sees CRISPR as a way to treat diseases and improve the food we eat (by creating traits in plants that reduce the need for chemical fertilizers and pesticides). But her discovery is a double-edged sword. It could potentially allow scientists to edit not just diseases, but also any human trait they choose, from eye color to intelligence level. And that's the kind of stuff that inspires scary dystopian novels about oddly perfect, robotic populations. As far as Jennifer's concerned, there's a difference between what *can* be done and what *should* be done. She's organized a hold among scientists on using CRISPR to modify human beings. She also heads the Innovative Genomics Institute in Berkeley, which weaves consideration of societal consequences right into its research.

ASKING FOR HELP

After announcing her groundbreaking discovery in a 2012 paper, Jennifer was overwhelmed by the response—literally. She said, "My inbox was exploding, and journal editors were calling me. It was just crazy. You could see this tidal wave coming towards you, you know?" She felt exhausted, and the craziness had only just begun. That's when her sister Ellen gave her some sage advice: ask for help. Over the next several years, Jennifer would hire a full team of people to help her manage her professional life and maintain balance in her personal life. When you design your life, you can do it all. You just can't do it all by yourself. Never be too proud to ask for help!

A self-proclaimed former geek and outcast, Jennifer saw her popularity skyrocket. She was invited to star-studded galas, consulted on movies, gave a TED Talk, and even addressed Congress. And she continued to run multiple companies, attend conferences, teach and mentor students, and do the work that inspires her—finding even better gene editors than Cas9. "I love the science," she says. "When I wake up in the morning, that's the first thing I'm thinking about, and when I go to bed at night, that's usually the last thing I'm thinking about."

Today, Jennifer continues to find new ways to shape her life and balance all of the demands on her time. Luckily, she's built up a battery of smart, capable, and empowered students to help do research, run her companies, and attend events in her place. And for her, watching her students succeed is the most rewarding part of the life she's designed. "In the end, it's really about creating a future for science. And the future is the people that we train, and the people that they go on and train. That's really what it's all about for me."

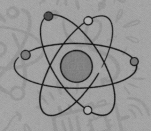

"SCIENCE MAKES PEOPLE REACH SELFLESSLY *for* TRUTH AND OBJECTIVITY; *it teaches people to accept reality, with* WONDER AND ADMIRATION, *not to mention the* DEEP AWE AND JOY *that the natural order of things brings to* THE TRUE SCIENTIST."

—LISE MEITNER, PHYSICIST